PERFORMANCE

EMI
Architekt*innen
Edelaar
Mosayebi
Inderbitzin

AF086686

The three authors who have contributed to this publication fulfilled a variety of roles in the featured projects. Laurent Stalder lent his support to our discussions relating to the Jungfrau East Ridge competition, Nina Zschocke, having been a test resident in the apartment mock-up at ETH, brings firsthand experience, while Joseph Schwartz played a pivotal role in the structural calculations for the performative fabric installation at the Swiss Art Awards.

Concept: EMI Architekt*innen AG, Edelaar, Mosayebi, Inderbitzin
Project management: Katharina Sommer
Translations: Fiona Elliott, David Koralek, Catherine Schelbert
Copy editing and proofreading: Louise Stein
Design: NORM, Zurich
Lithography, printing and binding: Druckerei Odermatt AG, Dallenwil
Paper: Profimatt, 150 g/m² and Profibulk 1.1, 60 g/m²

© 2025 EMI Architekt*innen AG and Park Books AG, Zurich
© for the texts: the authors
© for the images: the photographers
1 | 11–13: Gunnar Meier
2 | 11–13 and 16–23: Roland Bernath, 14/15: EMI Architekt*innen
3 | 11–18: Roland Bernath
4 | 11–15: EMI Architekt*innen, 16–18: Roland Bernath

All rights reserved; no part of this publication may be reproduced, stored in a retrieval system or transmitted in any form or by any means, electronic, mechanical, photocopying, recording, or otherwise, without the prior written consent of the publisher.

Park Books AG
Niederdorfstrasse 54, 8001 Zurich, Switzerland
www.park-books.com, +41 44 262 16 62, info@park-books.com
Park Books is being supported by the Federal Office of Culture with a general subsidy for the years 2021–2025.

ISBN 978-3-03860-337-5

Product safety
Responsible person pursuant to EU Regulation 2023/988 (GPSR):
GVA Gemeinsame Verlagsauslieferung Göttingen GmbH & Co. KG
Post Box 2021, 37010 Göttingen, Germany
+49 551 384 200 0, info@gva-verlage.de

ARCHITECTURE OF PERFORMANCE
RON EDELAAR, ELLI MOSAYEBI, CHRISTIAN INDERBITZIN

The term "performance" is generally used in connection with the performance capability of a machine or with reference to an artistic presentation in the form of a live event or happening.[1] Its technical and artistic aspects explain its particular appeal in architectural discourse. When applied in architecture "performance" opens up a potential not only for variability and versatility but also for the individualized treatment of space and its architectural elements.

However, a distinction should be drawn between the term "performance" and the idea of flexibility. *Merriam-Webster* associates "flexible" with things that are "characterized by [a] ready capability for modification or change, by plasticity, pliancy, variability, and often by consequent adaptability to new situations." Flexibility signifies adaptation to external pressure. Following its occurrence that adaptation is final—at least for a certain time.[2] By contrast "performance" suggests change from within. These transformations are never final, they are ongoing. The aim of "performance" lies in change itself. Thus, the impulse for change is intrinsic to the concept of "performance"—with lingering echoes of the capacities of machinery. While flexibility responds to economic or functional pressures, performance embodies pleasure, entertainment, and the expansion of possibilities.

In the theory of the aesthetics of theatrical performance, the relevant space is described as a *fixed* container that only turns into a performative space by virtue of the performance taking place within it. On one hand, "the space in which a performance takes place represents an architectural-geometric space." It has "a specific ground plan, measures a certain height, breadth, length, volume, and is fixed and stable." On the other hand, "the space in which a performance occurs can be regarded as a performative space." It is an "unstable and fluctuating space. The performance's spatiality is brought forth by the performative space and must be examined within the parameters set by it."[3]

In our performative projects the space itself changes. That space is far from rigidly geometric: on the contrary it becomes an actor and hence an active participant in its (own) performance. Additional performative elements such as shifting light, sound, human movements and actions enrich the performativity of the moment. The "special possibilities" that arise between recipients and actors, as described by Fischer-Lichte, may thus be even more intense, because the distinction between

---

[1] We arrived at this interpretation of performance through a comment made by Laurent Stalder in a lecture he gave at the guest studio *Ruinen und Maschinen* at ETH Zurich (2017–18).

[2] Sigrid Loch distinguishes between three forms of flexibility. Her notion of "integrated flexibility" has a lot in common with our idea of "performance". As she puts it: "Due to this option to 'increase space' this [integrated flexibility] has a special potential for enhancing and improving the functional value of small residential units, particularly in housing for the elderly. It enables space-saving, multiple uses and can simultaneously improve domestic comfort and living." Sigrid Loch, *Das adaptive Habitat, Typologie und Bedeutungswandel flexibler Wohnmodelle*. Dissertation for the faculty of Architecture and Urban Planning, Universität Stuttgart, 2009, Stuttgart: Universität Stuttgart, Institut Wohnen und Entwerfen, 2011, p. 2.

[3] Erika Fischer-Lichte, *The Transformative Power of Performance: A New Aesthetics*, trans. by Saskya Iris Jain, Oxford: Routledge, 2008, p. 107.

the latter is rendered obsolete. All the actors are fully engaged and in the midst of things.

Performative Space
A performative space is a variable space that changes as it interacts with human beings. Working with ETH students and the scenographer Selina Puorger, we designed and constructed two spatial installations with mobile spaces that encourage movement in their users. The spatial principle of the installation was based on the idea of diverging pairs of concepts and hence on the simultaneity of opposing or very different attributes. As a consequence, space should not be conceived of as a rigid vessel but rather as a fluid body that alternates between conflicting states.

In the first installation, *Un-Vorhersehbar* (Un-Foreseeable), there are four walls that can be set to create very different spatial conditions—confined and compressed or open and wide. The second installation, *Zyklisch-Konstant* (Cyclical-Constant), consists of a low-hanging square ceiling that presses downward, keeping the height of the space down to two meters. The ceiling slowly rotates around its own central axis. Beneath the ceiling there is a wall (containing the space on one side) and a triangular mirrored object. These isolated elements are united by a rotating, flying light in the corner of the ceiling. This pinpoint of light comes into view like a small sun, only to disappear again behind the wall, causing the foreground and the background of the construction to light up in turn.[4]

The idea of a fluid, changeable, fluctuating space is closely connected with the theory of a "second modernity."[5] Zygmunt Bauman proclaimed fluidity as the metaphor of the present day: "Fluids, so to speak, neither fix space nor bind time. While solids have clear spatial dimensions but neutralize the impact, and thus downgrade the significance, of time (effectively resist its flow or render it irrelevant), fluids do not keep to any shape for long and are constantly ready (and prone) to change it; and so for them it is the flow of time that counts, more than the space they happen to occupy: that space, after all, they fill but 'for a moment'. In a sense, solids cancel time; for liquids, on the contrary, it is mostly time that matters. When describing solids, one may ignore time altogether; in describing fluids, to leave time out of account would be a grievous mistake. Descriptions of fluids are all snapshots, and they need a date at the bottom of the picture."[6]

Fluidity, in Bauman's view, can thus only be recognized and comprehended with reference to time. Moreover, time and temporal changes are more important than space, which—unlike all that is fluid—articulates the principle of "solidity." Here Baumann defines space and time as two different principles, distinguishing between solid and fluid entities. Surprisingly, the possibility of conceiving of spaces as fluid is notably absent in Baumann's thinking. Yet that is precisely what does occur in a performative space: that which is solid becomes fluid, the space itself is set in motion.

Furthermore, performative spaces have their own "proper time" (*Eigenzeit*).[7] Through the way that they (can) change, they structure and "deepen" time and one's awareness of time. Gradual or rapid changes create intense, memorable moments and experiences. In that situation space and time engage in a dynamic interaction. In the extreme case spatial boundaries can only be perceived due to temporal changes.

In our work we have found various approaches to the idea of "performance", ranging from the technological machine metaphor in the Jungfrau East Ridge project to the theatrical mise-en-scène of anthropomorphisms and the transformability of spatial configurations in our residential building in Stampfenbachstrasse. The three projects featured in this publication all came into being during the course of the last twelve years. Their common denominator is our aim to treat change and mutation, the solid and the fluid, time and proper time as integral to architecture.

A Clockwork House (2012–)
Our project *Clockwork House* (still in the planning stage) to create a tourist destination on the East Ridge of the Jungfrau derives its performative character from the direct use of a machine metaphor in its architecture. The basis of the project is a now defunct directional beam station at an altitude of around 3,600 meters above sea level. The site is accessed via a tunnel cut into ice and rock from the Jungfraujoch, the terminus of the world famous Jungfrau railway, which itself travels through the Eiger and the Mönch after it has left Kleine Scheidegg. The remit was to create a destination with viewing terraces, shops, restaurants, and an exhibition space for a special clock as a symbol of Switzerland.

However, rather than constructing an "exhibition space" for watches, we felt there was greater appeal in the idea of treating the architecture itself as a time piece—that is to say, designing a "clockwork building," because an architectural structure at this location has unique potential for creating a new connection between time

---

4 Our videos of dancers document the changing relationships between the body, space, perception, and effect. See https://mosayebi.arch.ethz.ch/en/models/
5 In particular the notion of "reflexive modernization" expounded by Ulrich Beck. He describes an epochal shift from a first to a second modernity by dint of development itself. While the first modernity was shaped by linearity and hence a hierarchical stratification of social classes and groups, in Beck's view the hallmark of the second modernity is reflexivity. He suggests that, through the interaction of science, technology, and industry, this is leading to the loss of boundaries and thus to unforeseeable risks—as exemplified in climate change. Thesis 5 of the "Twelve Theses on the Architecture of the Second Modernity" (https://mosayebi.arch.ethz.ch/en/twelve-theses/) proposes that we think in dichotomies, because unintended side effects are constantly undermining our actions and intentions. Thinking in dichotomies was the basis for the development of fluid or performative spatial situations.
6 Zygmunt Bauman, *Liquid Modernity*, Cambridge: Polity Press, 2000, p. 2.
7 Helga Nowotny, *Eigenzeit Revisited*, 30 September 2015, https://mediathek.hkw.de/en/video/helga-nowotny---eigenzeit-revisited--englisch-?q=helga-nowotny&backscreen=search&overlayObjectType=audio&overlayObjectSlug=eigenzeit-revisited---helga-nowotny--englisch-

and space. We discussed the cosmic associations that arise here as one gazes out into the universe: the speed of light, the movements of the sun, the stars, and the planets. The architecture highlights these associations not only by virtue of the view from there but also by translating and visualizing them in the clockwork.

The outcome is a kinetic architectural design that creates its own time-space experience. The building-sized clockwork mechanism takes the form of a classic, pendulum clock, which in this case runs on wind power and is thus self-sufficient. The moving parts of the clock are designed as spaces that visitors can enter as they proceed on a *promenade architecturale* through the clockwork and experience time in terms of space, sound, and touch. Two realms—the mechanism (the function of time) and the display (the legibility of time)—become one. The mechanism also has an impact on the façade, opening and closing it according to the rhythms of time: the clock movement thus choreographs a sequence of changing views with shifting light and shade. At night the clockwork building can only be discerned from afar by its slowly pulsating light.

Anthropomorphic Form (2019–21)
The installation *Anthropomorphic Form*, created for the Swiss Art Awards exhibition in 2021, consisted of a fabric ceiling that extended the full length of the exhibition hall, transforming it into a new architectural space. At first sight it called to mind temporary structures such as festival marquees, although that impression was then quickly dispelled because the fabric was constantly in motion, changing its shape.

The translucent fabric was suspended on thin cables aligned along five axes, with each cable connected to one of forty-two motors. The motors were controlled by an algorithm that processed various aspects of human activity and atmospheric conditions: noise levels, the number and distribution of visitors, the speed of their movements, and so on. The fabric ceiling thus in effect became an organ of the visitors in attendance and almost imperceptibly created ever-changing spatial backdrops to the architectural exhibition—sometimes monumental, sometimes intimate, now architectural, now organic. At one moment the fabric formed the roof of an archaic tented pavilion, at another it swathed the gathering in a mimetic cloud.[8]

Performative House (2018—22)
In the *Performative House* we translated an interactive space into lived-in architecture. In response to a commission to construct a block of small apartments on Stampfenbachstrasse, we set about creating homes that would supersede "downsized" family apartments and simple one-room lofts. The idea behind this kind of living is based on the notion of a "performative space" that specifically adapts to its occupants or can be adjusted by them. It wraps around the human body like a garment: it can be opened and closed; it has various "pockets" and storage spaces for everyday household items. With a non-rectilinear floor plan all the walls are set in motion. In reality there are three movable elements: a pivot wall, a pivot cupboard, and two pivot lamps.

We designed the pivoting elements in such a way that there are no fixed positions: their movements are fluid and open. Handles invite the occupants to take hold of an item and move it. There are chunky, painted kitchen handles, metal plates for the pivot wall and the pivot cupboard, glass knobs for the bathroom door, and car seat belts for the swing-arm lamps and the platform drawers. The occupants push, turn, pull, and bend down. Large mirrors on the moving elements enhance their interactions with space, perception, and utilization.

Two platforms in niches in the apartment serve as horizontal cupboards and provide additional storage space. They also serve as furniture: mattresses and cushions can be placed directly on them. Here we make reference to traditions in Japan and the Far East.

Before the design was finally realized, a mock-up of a typical apartment was evaluated at ETH Zurich. The prototype occupied a spot on the roof of the HIL building for over a year and hosted both single occupants and couples.[9]

Caccia
Many years ago we had already identified the mutual impact of motion, patterns of movement, and spatial variations in the work of the Milanese architect Luigi Caccia Dominioni. We were particularly fascinated by the dual figuration of movable and moving.[10] In the mid-1950s Caccia was already replacing static, rectilinear spatial structures with flowing, movable, continuous spaces. He conceived the home as a horizontal, never-ending spatial sculpture, in which greater importance attaches to the actual areas of movement than, for instance, to the bedroom and bathroom which he regarded as static areas of retreat. Exploratory lines in numerous sketches of floor plans show Caccia assuming the role of future users, so as to anticipate potential patterns of movement. Caccia presumed a mutually influential relationship between people and space. The space is set in motion, in the same way that shifting spatial conditions set people in motion.

A special element on the cusp between daily use and theatrical staging is that of the door. Caccia often specified full-height, lacquered, reflective double doors for his interiors. However, they are not inserted into the wall as cut-outs with frames and lintels, but are hinged directly to the floor and the ceiling. The space is energized by

---

8   EMI Architekt*innen realized this project together with Fabian Bircher. The project director was Lukas Burkhart.

9   The report and evaluation of this research project (2019–21) are available on: https://mosayebi.arch.ethz.ch/en/research/. Scroll down to "vacancy – no vacancy. A performative house of the future."

10   Elli Mosayebi, "Wege und Räume. Wohnungen von Luigi Caccia Dominioni," in *werk, bauen + wohnen*, 3/2005, pp. 12–17.

1
Apartment Building Stampfenbachstrasse, Zurich, 2018–22, standard floor plan

2
Vacancy – no vacancy, mock-up, ETH Zurich, 2019–21, floor plan with lines marking the movements of performative elements

3–5
A Clockwork House, Jungfrau East Ridge, competition entry, 2012, 1st Prize, floor plans for levels 3 and 4; cross section

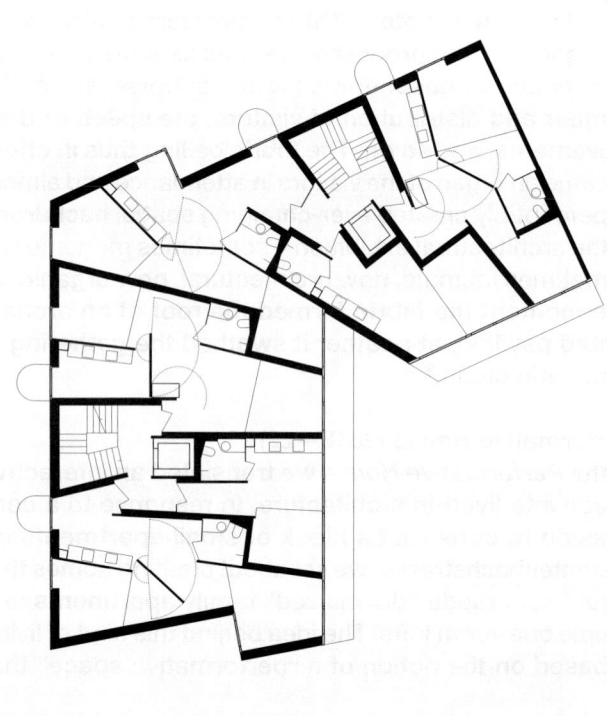

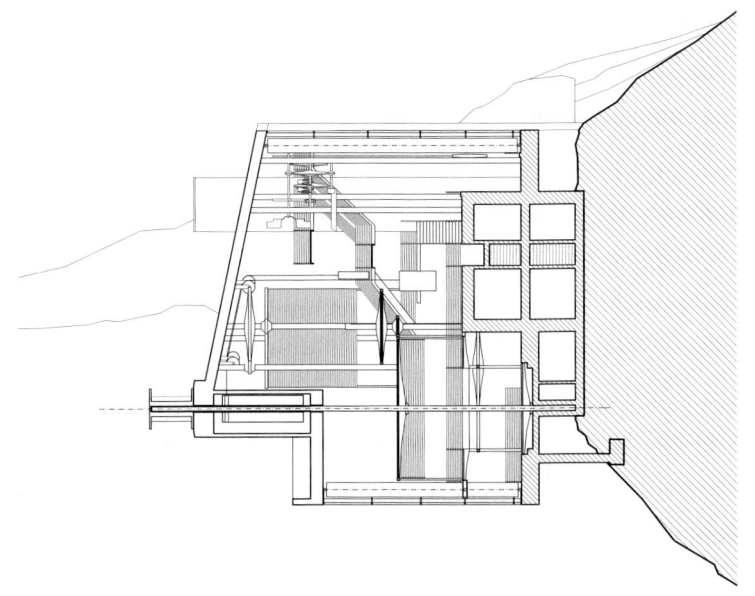

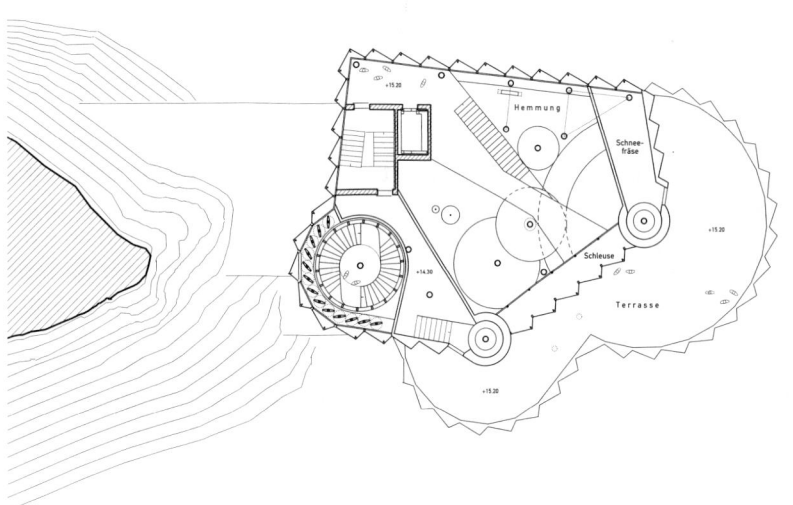

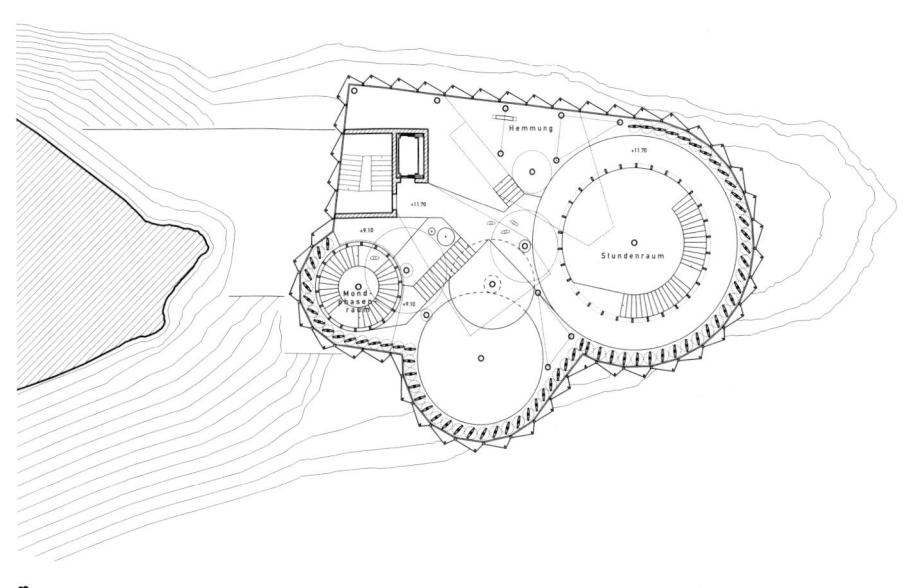

the optical impact of these lacquered doors, and reflections create virtual enfilades that appear to extend the physically restricted space.

A preference for "dissolving" walls and creating a somewhat more open floor plan is also seen in the work of other architects and developers from Milan. Possibly the most beautiful example of this is the experimental wall construction by Angelo Mangiarotti that was featured in *Domus* in 1952: it consists of a row of rotatable panels with abstract compositions painted on both sides of them by the American artist William Klein. The description of this as a *costruzione infinita* references the endless ways of changing the space by resetting the panels—the article in *Domus* cites 140 variants.[11]

Doors as Performative Figures

Doors play an important part as performative elements in many of the projects we have developed in our practice.[12] In the residential building on Geibelstrasse, for instance, doors serve as a performative figure that regulates and shapes spatial connections. Certain internal doors are combined here with a pair of French doors, forming a three-leaved unit. This unit thus determines not only the spatial relationship between two internal rooms but also the connection between inside and outside. If all three doors are closed then the connection is limited to a flat view of the outside world through a window that is angled inward. If all three doors are open, an open spatial configuration ensues that extends the lens-like outside space into the inside space. This orientates the interior on a diagonal to the narrow street and prevents any frontal confrontation with the houses on the other side.

By contrast, certain doors in our apartment block on Freihofstrasse are installed in a comedic arrangement. Each apartment has a central kitchen-dining room, from which all the other rooms can be accessed. The proposal was that the living room could be closed off and used as an additional bedroom. This explains the notable compartmentalization of the floor plan and the uniformity of the rooms. They all have similar dimensions and can be closed off by a door.

Yet the rooms are not undifferentiated—they are distinguished by their doors. This is noticeable in the pair of doors in the back wall of the kitchen, opening into the two rooms beyond it. One door extends from floor to ceiling and is relatively narrow, whereas the door immediately next to it has a lintel and is wider. With the obvious difference in their dimensions each of the doors develops its own anthropomorphic appearance. This is reinforced by the door handles being mounted at different heights.

In the same way that columns were not only given human proportions but also had "human characters" attributed to them, these doors develop their own individual characters. We compared this pair of doors to Laurel and Hardy: two highly expressive figures that are not memorable for their elegance but rather for their whimsy and eccentricity. These are anthropomorphic forms that the apartment's occupants can identify with.

Yet another different relationship between room, wall, and door is found in the apartment building on Steinwiesstrasse. In this case the composition of the volumes and the floor plans are based on artistic principles that obey a situational logic. The interiors of the apartments are underpinned by a notional pathway that leads the occupants from "inside" to "outside." The open fireplace in the outdoor living room is the focal point of that route. The spaces that unfold along that route resemble the successive scenarios that we know from landscape gardens. The solid walls, guiding the occupants' movements, frame and open up different views out into the garden. The doorways are finished with high lintels in such a way that the continuity and planarity of the guiding walls is not destroyed. Once again there is movement within a layout that is not determined by functional necessity but rather by the idea of a flâneur.

Performance

The projects outlined here demonstrate our interest in architecture that liberates itself not only from physical and structural limitations but also from any passive function as a neutral backdrop. Through its adaptability, its appropriation and identification, space becomes its own protagonist, an opponent, a dancer, and an instrument. Immobility gives way to mobility as the architecture moves its users in multiple ways. Ultimately, it revolves around the aesthetic dimension of physical perception and handling.

---

11 Lisa Licitra Ponti, "Costruzione infinita," in *Domus*, 268 (1952), pp. 31–33.
12 See our essay on doors: Elli Mosayebi and Christian Inderbitzin, "La porte, une échelle de l'habitat," in *matières*, 13 (2016), pp. 86–97.

2|19

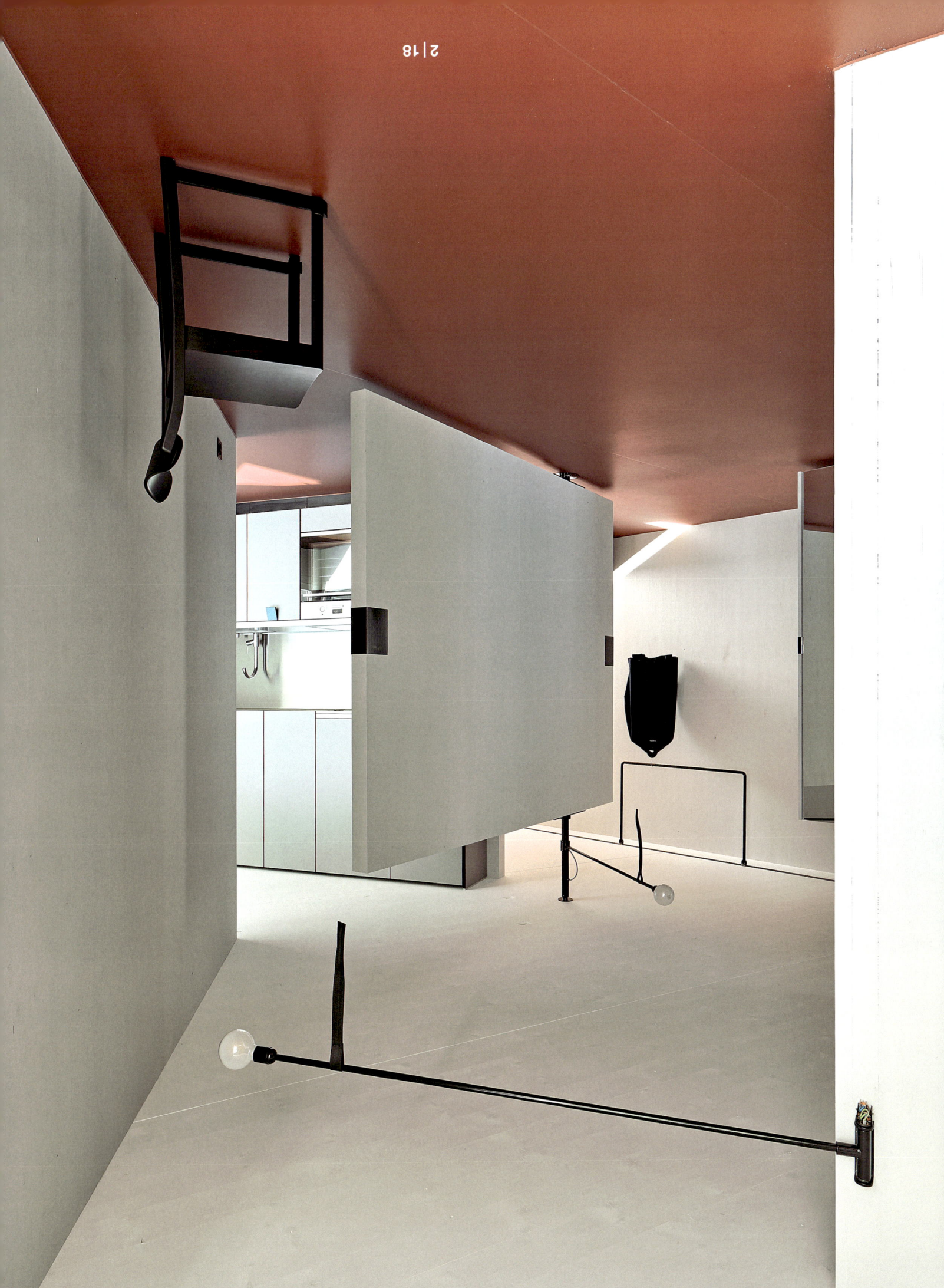

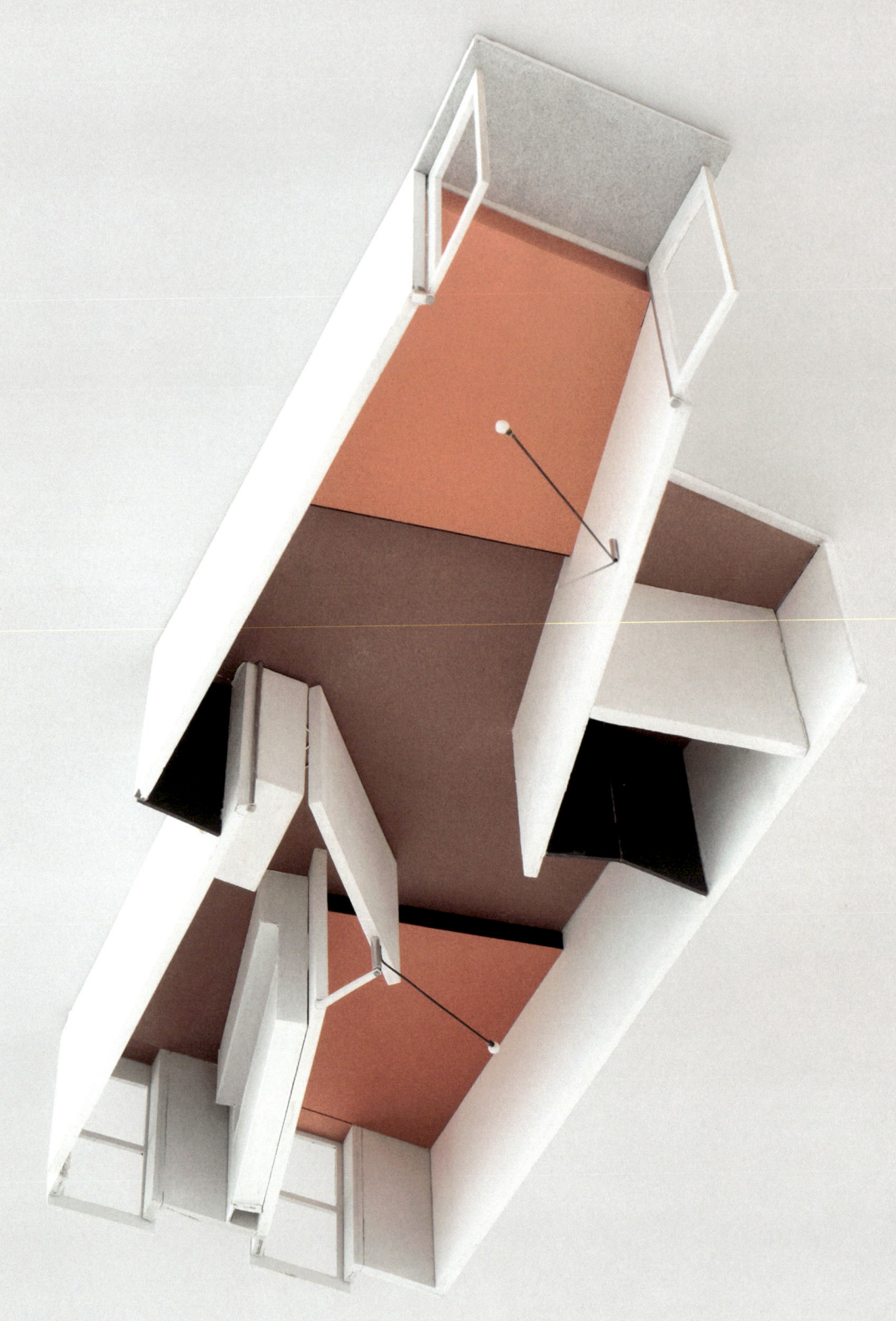

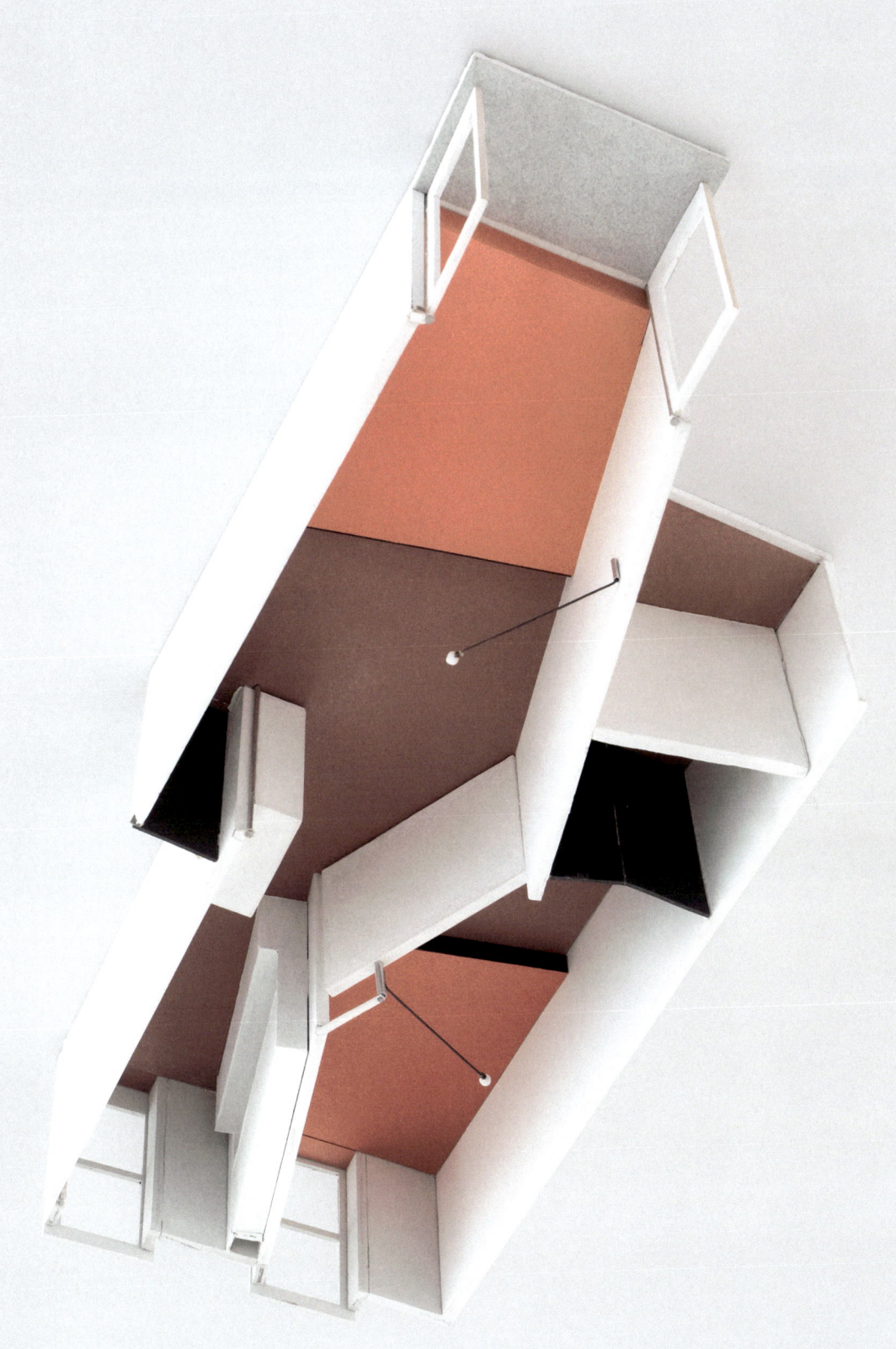

experiment and daily life come to terms? Can we as potential occupants reliably engineer the sequence of programs—or do the movements of the kinetic elements remain unpredictable and disconnected? Structured daily schedule or chaos, unpredictability, chance and play after all?

In any case, there are too many of us at the first viewing of the building on Stampfenbachstrasse in August 2022: too great is the interest in this new experiment in residential housing by EMI Architects.[39] But we do catch sight of details the mock-up did not have: clothes racks on rails or charming round shutters that can be "unfurled" to cover the illuminated bathroom window like the earth's shadow in an eclipse. The function of the kinetic wall in the small unit in which I am standing now changes: it pushes people more or less voluntarily from one part of the apartment to the other, like a revolving door moved collectively, one might say, and therefore difficult to control individually. There may well be witty, unanticipated consequences at future parties in these tiny households: the architecture itself invites us to dance and, in the process, reshuffles the temporary social arrangement!

---

39   For a representation of the residential building, ready for occupancy, see the architects' website: https://www.emi-architekten.ch/en/projects/stampfenbach/. See also: https://performatives-haus.ch/

were extremely curious to find out whether it would be of any use and what it would reveal.[27]

Subsequent evaluation showed that, as anticipated, the flexible elements served primarily to accommodate different needs by day and night.[28] In addition, 39 percent of the test subjects wanted the rotating wall to be smaller or hinged so that it could be temporarily stowed away.[29] The fact that neither size nor position of the rotating wall has changed in the units at Stampfenbachstrasse reflects the will of the project designers. The spatial layout never comes to a standstill since the wall always obstructs potential movement through the apartment in one direction or another—in other words, it has be rotated out of the way. Thanks to the rotating wall, the mock-up and its later variations belong to the field of:

Kinetics.

"Everything moves. There is no standstill."[30] Or: "Movement. Nothing is constant, everything keeps changing."[31] As of the mid-20th century, these and similar programmatic statements motivated artistic interest in the phenomenon of motion and in making kinetic works.[32] Rolf Glasmeier used elements of architecture or interior fittings for his *Kaufhaus Objekte* [Department Store Objects], such as mass-produced light switches that he purchased in department stores or window handles with which he made reliefs that can be manipulated, inviting visitors to "fiddle with them".[33] Glasmeier also described his viewers as "players."[34] Like the intuitive interaction with elements that can be swiveled and rotated in the mock-up, elements of everyday life in art may also encourage a spontaneous play of variations. Formally, however, the flexible floor plan of *vacancy – no vacancy* reminds me even more of Gerhard von Graevenitz's kinetic wall objects, with strips of metal or wood made to rotate by a hidden electric motor. Often, several elements in an image will appear to move independently. The core concern in these serial variations is the relationship between programming and chance or between chaos and order. The works thus show complex systematics, but also

asymmetries, loosely devised mechanical hinges and always playful experiments with variations on compositions of simple graphic elements. Although abstract, the seemingly disorderly, spontaneous dance of dark strips rotating on a light background generates the impression of animated interplay.

The interplay of von Graevenitz's kinetic elements is always smooth even when they overlap. Not so Ralf Baecker's complex relief of 2018, in which 1250 small white, rotating slats against a black background react upon making contact and become temporarily stabilized. With a different focus than that of von Graevenitz, namely, the complex action of independent electro mechanic motors, Baecker also investigates the random and ordered systemic behavior of spontaneously formed patterns. According to the artist, "PTPBTA acts as an epistemological instrument to look at dynamics that emerge from non-hierarchical and collective organizations/systems which can be found in many areas and on different scales like social systems, economics, climate system, and biology."[35] This wide arc of comparison from system to aesthetics, though rather abstract or schematic, does take me back to the movable, space-defining elements of the mock-up created by the Mosayebi chair.[36] They, too, may collide physically or express friction between occupants of the unit.[37] Like every kinetic object, the movable elements of the apartment are also displays: even without sensors, they map the forces that move them and reveal the specific moment of living in the apartment. That applies to the building on Stampfenbachstrasse as well, where no sensors have been installed in the numerous small units. When I imagine the building as a whole with its multitude of movable walls, it seems to me like a complex but enigmatic three-dimensional display. Is this complex of apartments a kind of clock? And if so, what does it indicate? What kind of information would this building give us with all of its kinetic elements if all the arrangements were visible from outside? Circulation, spatial and physical performances, closings, openings, collisions and compromises, but also: working conditions and their rhythm, social configurations or even the emotional state of the residents?[38] Can the will to

---

27   The writer in conversation with Elli Mosayebi in the mock-up, 22 April 2021. For a subsequent report and evaluation of the data, see, for instance: https://mosayebi.arch.ethz.ch/vacancy/index.html

28   https://vacancy-questionnaire.web.app/, 3.3 Räumliche Situationen im Mock-Up, die durch die Testpersonen hergestellt wurden [Spatial situations created in the mock-up by test occupants].

29   https://vacancy-questionnaire.web.app/, 6.2 [Wie würden die Testpersonen die beweglichen Elemente verbessern? Drehwand verkleinern und/oder verstaubar gestalten. [How would the test occupants improve the movable elements? Decrease size of rotating wall and/or design it to be put away.]

30   Jean Tinguely, *Für Statik*, March 1959, manifesto, distributed as a flyer from an airplane above Düsseldorf. See: https://www.tinguely.ch/de/ahoy/mt-ahoy/tinguely-history/duesseldorf.html

31   Ludwig Wilding, *Visuelle Phänomene* (ex. cat. Museum für Konkrete Kunst Ingolstadt), Cologne: Wienand, 2007, p. 18.

32   On the universalized viewer and the idea of a global aesthetic in kinetic art, see also: Nina Zschocke, "Ludwig Wilding," in: *Highlights 01. 5 Jahre Stiftung für Konkrete Kunst und Design* (exh. cat. Museum für Konkrete Kunst Ingolstadt), Cologne: Wienand, 2012, pp. 9–15.

33   Glasmeier, quoted in: Frederik Schikowski, "Anmerkungen zu Rolf Glasmeiers variablen Arbeiten," in: *Künstler der Stiftung für Konkrete Kunst und Design Ingolstadt* (exh. cat. Museum für Konkrete Kunst Ingolstadt), Cologne: Wienand, 2017, pp. 34–37, here p. 34.

34   Ibid., p. 35.

35   Ralf Baecker, *Putting The Pieces Back Together Again. Autonomous System*, 2018. See: https://rlfbckr.io/work/ptpbta/. See also Baecker's lecture at a conference on digital materiality organized by Fabio Gramazio and Nina Zschocke, 9 April 2022, ETH Zurich, See: https://video.ethz.ch/events/2022/materiality.html

36   For systems aesthetics, see e.g.: B. Inge Hinterwaldner: *Das systemische Bild. Ikonizität im Rahmen computergestützter Echtzeitsimulationen*, Munich: Wilhelm Fink, 2010, esp. pp. 103–105. The term goes back to: Jack Burnham, "Systems Esthetics," in: *Artforum*, Sept. 1968, pp. 30–35. Archived at: https://www.artforum.com/print/196807/systems-esthetics-32466

37   The radius of movement of the rotating wall and the bathroom door overlap in the mock-up. For example, in some of the apartments at Stampfenbachstrasse, the wall does not rotate entirely past the kitchen. On potential friction among occupants, see https://vacancy-questionnaire.web.app/, 5.2. Kamen sich die Testpersonen bei der Benutzung der beweglichen Elemente in die Quere? [Did the occupants get in one another's way while using the movable elements?] 23 percent of the two-person groups answered the question positively and 75% negatively.

38   For considerations in response to the data collected in the mock-up and related questions, see: Prof. Dr. Elli Mosayebi and Julia Hemmerling: *Performatives Haus, Auswertung 2019–2022*, ETH Zurich 2022. See: https://backend.mosayebi.arch.ethz.ch/site/assets/files/1046/220911_performatives_haus_digital.pdf

inscribed in interactive environments—or deduced by subjects from environments or elements of environments.[18] The perception of this implicit invitation is multirelational, that is, it occurs only within specific relational configurations. It might be said that people with their goals and needs lock into environments (including machines) in order to make them function for their own use. In consequence, they not only set them in motion, but are themselves set in motion as well.

In contrast to the optimization of production procedures proposed by Taylor—a classical example applied to the home environment is Margarete Schütte-Lihotzky's Frankfurt Kitchen—the flexible elements in the mock-up do not define any ideal sequences of action; instead, these arise out of the play between the spatial elements and the needs of the occupants or the fun of testing and trying things out, especially on the first encounter. The rotating wall is also an obstruction; it stands in the way and because it has to be shifted to access other areas, it indicates the movements of the occupants. Through hidden sensors, the mock-up installed at ETH Zurich acquires the character of a laboratory. Measuring the movement of the furniture indicates how occupants use the space. According to Elli Mosayebi, the behavioral studies are aimed at understanding to what extent occupants are willing to live with and implement change.[19] Sensors were attached not only to the experimental, rotating elements of the interior design but also to more conventional furnishings such as the doors of the overhead kitchen cabinets, the refrigerator, the garbage can, and the drawers. The architects were interested in which elements are manipulated when, which adjustments are made when, how often they were changed and whether there were observable differences between user groups. An animated floor plan made it possible to subsequently call up all movements, week by week and day by day. A questionnaire inquired into the test occupants' own experiences and gave them the opportunity to add comments. Subsequent evaluation shows quantitative measurements and data in graphs, pie charts, and bar charts.[20]

Knowing that data is being collected, that I am being measured, impacts my experience as a test occupant in the mock-up. Everyday activities are latently geared toward the gaze of others, in this case the absent but watching makers of the project, albeit indirectly through the sensors. Even if collected data and feedback serve to evaluate the test building—or rather the performative play between spatial elements and occupants—am I not

also being tested and my behavior evaluated for future productions?[21] Am I "responsive enough to change"? And how can that actually be measured?

At first sight, the apartment, fitted with sensors, is reminiscent of experiments in psychology, such as those conducted in behavioral psychology. The so-called Skinner box or operant conditioning chamber, devised by B. F. Skinner, is a special kind of interactive minimal habitat.[22] Constructed of simple elements, it is nonetheless a "clever apparatus": an empty space equipped with stimulus, input and output interfaces. For Skinner, a laboratory, generally speaking, is a place where "conditions are simplified and irrelevant conditions often eliminated. But [...] we can gain control over behavior only insofar as we can control the factors responsible for it. [...] The laboratory simplification reveals the relevance of factors which we might otherwise overlook."[23] Further, Skinner explains that "the experimental method includes the use of instruments which improve our *contact* with behavior and with the variables of which it is a *function*."[24] The use of recording devices enables researchers "to observe behavior over long periods of time, and accurate recording and measurement make effective quantitative analysis possible."[25] In the behaviorist laboratory, clearly defined manipulation of variables underlies research into the significance of specific conditions of behavior: "The most important feature of the laboratory method is the deliberate manipulation of variables: the importance of a given condition is determined by changing it in a controlled fashion and observing the result."[26] In Skinner's experimental laboratory, behavior is therefore studied by shaping behavior through controlled decision-making architecture and reward systems.

However, *vacancy – no vacancy* is not a behaviorist conditioning machine nor is it a cybernetic control system. Test subjects receive a reward or, more generally, feedback, at most through the generated spatial configurations—or purely by imagining how their behavior is evaluated. Moreover, the collected data had no direct impact on the design of the living spaces on Stampfenbachstrasse, the construction of which commenced while the mock-up was still in use. The collection of the data is essentially a test run rather than a rigorously scientific series of experiments. While it was still being collected, it was clear that the architects

---

18   James J. Gibson, *The Senses Considered as Perceptual Systems*, Boston: Houghton Mifflin, 1966; James J. Gibson: *The Ecological Approach to Visual Perception*, Boston: Houghton Mifflin, 1979; Edward Reed and Rebecca Jones, *Reasons for Realism: Selected Essays of James J. Gibson*, Hillsdale, London/New York: Routledge, 1982. Tim Ingold, for example, refers to Gibson's approach. See: Tim Ingold, *The Perception of the Environment. Essays on Livelihood, Dwelling and Skill*, London/New York: Routledge, 2000.

19   The writer in conversation with Elli Mosayebi in the mock-up, ETH Hönggerberg, 22 April, 2021.

20   Prof. Dr. Elli Mosayebi and Julia Hemmerling: *Performatives Haus, Auswertung 2019–2022*, ETH Zurich 2022, pp. 31ff., https://backend.mosayebi.arch.ethz.ch/site/assets/files/1046/220911_performatives_haus_digital.pdf

21   Sabeth Buchmann compares participative concepts of artistic performance with cybernetic feedback cycles and with the quantification procedures of corporate development (monitoring, reporting). Sabeth Buchmann, "Feed Back. Performance in der Bewertungsgesellschaft," in: *Texte zur Kunst*, no. 10, June 2018, pp. 35–53.

22   B. F. Skinner, *The behavior of organisms: An experimental analysis*, New York: Appleton-Century, 1938, pp. 48–49. https://archive.org/details/in.ernet.dli.2015.191112/page/n47/mode/2up

23   B. F. Skinner, *Science and Human Behavior* (1953), New York: The Free Press, 1965, p. 14.

24   Ibid., p. 37.

25   Ibid., p. 37.

26   Ibid., p. 37.

In her multivolume dissertation *Das Adaptive Habitat. Typologie und Bedeutungswandel flexibler Wohnmodelle*, Sigrid Loch of the Institute Housing and Design at the University of Stuttgart distinguishes two motives for developing flexible concepts: on one hand, the development of avant-garde spatial models and experimental housing concepts and on the other, planning for the existence minimum in the form of space-saving, overlapping uses as well as models for building and settlement growth in times of need, as in 1920s Germany.[11] The temporary mini-habitat—*vacancy – no vacancy*—on the roof of the Faculty of Architecture is also related to a need: Zurich is a city with no available affordable housing.

With 54.5 square meters of floor space, the Hönggerberg mock-up, like most of the housing units subsequently built, can accommodate one or, at most, two occupants. The building that EMI Architects designed on Stampfenbachstrasse contains small apartments ranging from 26 to 58 square meters and one larger unit on the ground floor. An actual increase in space can hardly be expected through the flexibility of the implemented kinetic architectural elements. While spatial proposals of the early 20th century—as a rule in response to exigencies (with the exception perhaps of El Lissitzky's)—ensured a "flexible encircling of necessary minimum areas" and also enabled overlapping uses for the transition between night and day, the Zurich model house primarily enables playful variations of the spatial relationships.[12] As architect Elli Mosayebi puts it, "The floor area [of the mock-up] corresponds to a regular two-room apartment. Our aim was comfort and variability which has little to do with efficiency and flexibility. The usefulness of movable and mechanical elements is secondary. More importantly, it's fun [...]."[13] This type of apartment has long distanced itself from the conventional, mono-functional rooms and patterns of living that once typified the ideal of an industrial society with its bourgeois notion of the nuclear family. It is designed exclusively for singles or couples as a social entity. Moreover, by abandoning the monofunctional use of rooms, self-employed or dependent teleworkers can connect—or temporarily separate—working and living spaces. This living-working cell with kinetic divider is not primarily a response to individual needs but rather an expression of overall change in social life and working conditions. Maurizio Lazzarato already coined the term "immaterial labor" in the 1990s[14] and the multiuse of times and spaces with respect to work and recreation was, of course, accelerated by the COVID-19 pandemic

and the ongoing development of data infrastructure with the option of working from home. In the mock-up, the wall can instantly appear in the background to conceal the bed in the case of an incoming video call—and then moved again to open up the room after the teleconference.

The small apartment also suits the mobility required by the labor market since practically no additional furnishings are required as it is partially furnished and provides integrated storage. Here, too, precursors can be found, as in Andrea Zittel's work of the 1990s. The folding mechanisms of the *A-Z Living Units*, created by this pioneer of mobile and modular minimal housing, link several functions in the smallest of spaces, and the units can fold up like a steamer trunk to be moved to another location.[15] Interestingly, Zittel's work is not participative although the relationship between the self-empowerment of the artist as the designer of her own living environment and her serial, partially customized work for clients has to be renegotiated with each project. Similarly, the concept underlying the mock-up of the Mosayebi chair does not involve any cooperative design. Instead it offers:

Interactivity.
The mobile, spatially performative elements of the mock-up require no electronic technology; the unit has no computer-generated flexibility of the kind already envisioned in 1967 by Archigram under the influence of spaceship technology ("Living 1990," unbuilt design, later executed as a full-scale model).[16] Since the elements are moved by hand, the occupants engage in a physical performance with every modification of the space. In that respect, the folding and pushing movements of users in El Lissitzky's design already shows a theatrical tendency.[17] When the wall of EMI's mock-up rotates, occupants essentially dance along with it. Not only do the handles in the form of metal profiles on the wall and the flaps on the folding and swivel furniture invite interaction; the evident mobility of the elements is in itself an implicit invitation to interact. In his ecological theory of perception, James Gibson speaks of "affordance," by which he means the invitation to take action

---

11   Ibid., p. 35. Loch distinguishes between neutral spatial construction, renovation that enables "constructive flexibility," and "integrated flexibility" characterized by flexible room dividers.
12   On "encircling," see: ibid., p. 557.
13   Elli Mosayebi, quoted in: Palle Petersen, "Der bewegte Plan," in: *Hochparterre Blog*, 2. Sept. 2019, https://www.hochparterre.ch/nachrichten/architektur/der-bewegte-plan
14   On the essence and requirements of immaterial work, see: Maurizio Lazzarato, "Immaterial Labor," in: Paolo Virno und Michael Hardt, *Radical Thought in Italy: A Potential Politics*, Minneapolis, Minnesota/London: University of Minnesota Press, 1996, pp. 133–150.
15   Cf. https://www.zittel.org/projects/a-z-living-units
16   The history of media art distinguishes between interactivity, a concept oriented toward the technological relationship between human and machine that has gained traction since the 1990s, and older concepts of social interaction and—e.g., democratic—participation or creative collaboration which allows participants to intervene in and modify their environment. See: Dieter Daniels, "Strategien der Interaktivität," in: Rudolf Frieling, idem (eds), *Medien Kunst Interaktion – Die 80er und 90er Jahre in Deutschland*, Vienna/New York: Springer, 2000, pp. 142–169; Inke Arns, "Interaction, Participation, Networking: Art and Telecommunication," in: Rudolf Frieling and Dieter Daniels (eds), *Media Art Net 1. Overview of Media Art*, Vienna/New York: Springer, 2004, pp. 314–349; http://www.medienkunstnetz.de/themes/overview_of_media_art/communication/; Söke Dinkla, *Pioniere Interaktiver Kunst von 1970 bis heute*, Ostfildern: Hatje Cantz, 1997.
17   On the relationship between multi-functionality and theater in Russian constructivism, in particular El Lissitzky's wall mobile, see: Daniela Stöppel, "Falten, Klappen, Knicken als ästhetische Konzepte der Zwischenkriegszeit in Möbelgestaltung, Architektur und Grafikdesign," in: Rudolf Fischer and Wolf Tegethoff (eds), *Modern Wohnen. Möbeldesign und Wohnkultur der Moderne*, Berlin: Gebr. Mann Verlag, 2016, pp. 135–164, here p. 135; Katharina Hövelmann, *Bauhaus in Wien?*, Vienna/Cologne: Böhlau, 2021, https://doi.org/10.7767/9783205213161, pp. 208–209.

3
Andrea Zittel, *A–Z Living Unit*, 1994
Steel, wood, mattress, glass, mirror, lighting, hob, oven, velvet
open: 144.8 × 213.4 × 208.3 cm
closed: 93.3 × 213.4 × 96.5 cm
Courtesy the artist and Sprüth Magers

4
Gerhard von Graevenitz, *2 vertikale Streifen [2 Vertical Strips]*, 1977
Kinetic object, two movable metal bars on fiberboard, with electric motor
169 × 251 × 8 cm
Courtesy Galerie von Bartha, Private Collection Switzerland
© 2024, ProLitteris, Zurich

5
Rolf Glasmeier, *Kaufhaus Objekt [Department Store Object]*, 1971
Window handles on Resopal panel
26 × 26 × 7.5 cm
© 2024, ProLitteris, Zurich
Photograph: Rolf Glasmeier Archive

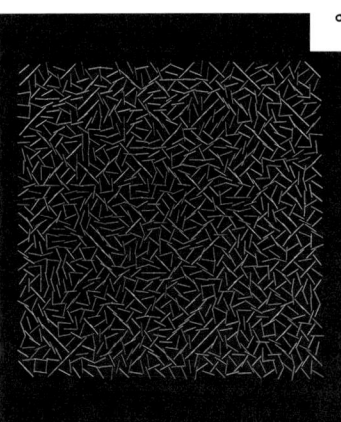

6
Ralf Baecker, *Putting the Pieces Back Together Again*, 2018
Installation view
Photograph: © Ralf Baecker

1

El Lissitzky, hinged partition for a communal dwelling, 1929
Illustrated in *Das neue Frankfurt: internationale Monatsschrift für die Probleme kultureller Neugestaltung*, Issue 11, November 1930, p. 245

2

Gio Ponti, studio apartment for four people, 1956
Courtesy Salvatore Licitra / Gio Ponti Archives

RUSSISCHE WOHNUNGSNOT UND IHRE LÖSUNGEN

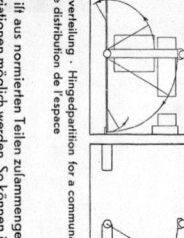

27 EL LISSITZKY, MOSKAU. Wandmobil für ein Kommunenhaus, 1929. Möglichkeiten der Raumverteilung. · Hingedpartition for a communalhouse, 1929. Possibilities of space distribution. · Paroi à gonds pour une maison communale, 1929. Possibilité de distribution de l'espace

Lißitzkys Vorschlag für ein „Wand-Mobil" in Wohnhaus-Kommunen

Diese möblierte, bewegliche Wand habe ich für die Typen des Kommunen-Hauses, die von dem Baukomitee des Ökonomie-Rates der R. S. F. S. R. aufgestellt wurden, erfunden.
An je einer der Eisenbetonstützen, die durch den Bau gehen, ist scharnierartig die Wand aufgehängt.

Die Wand selbst ist aus normierten Teilen zusammengestellt, so daß verschiedene Variationen möglich werden. So können in der Wand 1—3 Klappbetten enthalten sein; Arbeitstisch, Kleiderschrank, Spiegeltoilette usw.

El Lißitzky

28—29 Wandmobil · Hingedpartition · Paroi à gonds

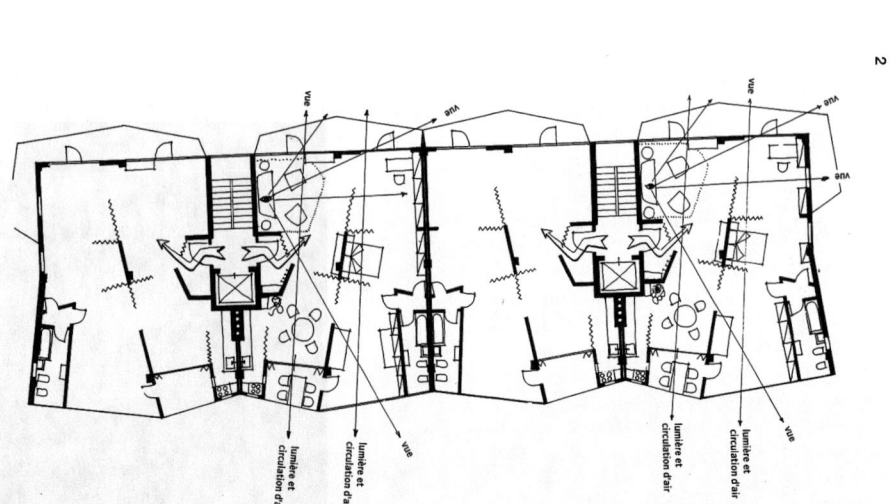

various subjects created in collaboration with the students.[3] For example, the course "Productive House" in spring 2019 worked out ideas for possible interior climates, taking into account various sources of power and heat as well as building materials. The second step in collaboration with scenographer Selina Puorger added backdrop and staging technology to the full-scale model. The primary aim was not inquiry into the energy features of the building but rather the study of lighting effects, surface aesthetics and also—thanks to invited dancers—a performative exploration of the space, especially as it potentially relates to the human body moving around within it.

Despite being executed in full-scale, stage sets as faux architecture or trompe-l'œil sculpture are ordinarily different from reality due to their materialization—a distinction that also applies to the students' preparatory projects. In addition, stage sets are ordinarily different front and back, one side is meant to be viewed, while the other is neglected. However, the mock-up on top of the architecture faculty does not make this distinction. In fact, the representation shifts into a borderline area where model and reality converge to the point of becoming indistinguishable. In an absurd short story of 1946, Jorge Luis Borges describes a "Map of the Empire whose size was that of the Empire, and which coincided point for point with it."[4] But a prototype does not follow its subject; it creates it to begin with, being, in principle, the original of a series that will later be implemented. At the same time, the model-like apartment transforms life inside it into a test of what will follow later. In any case, as a temporary occupant of the mock-up, I feel a slight alienation from the everyday elements and objects around me, and also from my own interaction with them—as if they were, in fact, barely distinguishable simulations of themselves.[5] Finally, the exposed location at my place of work and study contributes to the inner detachment from the intimate actions of cooking, living, sleeping. Every act is like a performance.

Being functionally different from its temporary location, the mock-up proves to be a fragment after all, namely, an isolated residential unit in an alien place. In addition, it is not a model of a one-family house that will go into serial production but rather a single model element of an apartment building projected for Stampfenbachstrasse in Zurich.[6] While the mock-up encroached like a little parasite on a larger building—where it required a structural support inserted into several stories of the building below—the project on Stampfenbachstrasse in Zurich groups the multiplied and varied units into a multilevel configuration, resting on the foundation of the preexisting building. The small test habitat presented the future mode of construction. It also demonstrated the proposed execution of the partially furnished apartment as:

Adaptive Habitat.
In the model apartment, closet and wall elements can be rotated around their own axis on a steel strut affixed to floor and ceiling. Every change of position modifies the relationship between cooking and living area. For example, the kitchen can be treated as separate from the combined living, working, and sleeping area. Or the bedroom might disappear behind the rotating wall so that it is concealed from the public kitchen and living areas. Positions in between define narrower passages and views. The variability of the mock-up's spatial arrangement makes it a "Performative Space,"[7] which has historical precedents, such as El Lissitzky's wall mobile for a commune[8]—an inserted element that could change position and serve as a closet as well as containing various items of foldout furniture. Here we already have the concept of users being given the option to interact with and construct space. Living and residing becomes a process, corresponding to a continuously changing habitat.[9] In comparison to Lissitzky's folding furniture inserted—or suspended from concrete supports—in a neutral space, the space in the mock-up by EMI Architects is more defined, despite kinetic flexibility, because of the permanently mounted furnishings. For her home E-1027 (Roquebrune-Cap-Martin, 1929), Eileen Gray also designed permanently installed, but flexible furniture that could be adjusted in relation to the body, in particular a swivel mirror, night table, and foldout desk. And finally, flexible spatial division (sliding or folding doors) to accommodate uses by day and by night was introduced, for instance by Carl Fieger (Berlin, Bauausstellung 1931)[10] or Gio Ponti in his unbuilt "one-room apartment for four people" designed 1956 for the journal *Domus*. Such designs permit a flexible response to social or personal needs as they change in the course of a day. The Hönggerberg mock-up clearly follows this line of thought.

---

3   In fall 2018: 1:1 model, performance, and filmed documentation: *Performativer Raum. Un-Vorhersehbar*, dancer: Reut Nahum, film: Sebastian Cantillo, lighting: Daniel Leuenberger, chair Prof. Dr. Elli Mosayebi, Lukas Burkhart, Theres Hollenstein, Nelly Pilz, Selina Puorger, https://vimeo.com/313403627; in spring 2019: design studio "Productive House," ETH Zurich, performance and filmed documentation: *Performative Space / Cyclic-Constant*. Dancers: Alex Jones, Michelle Willems; film: Sebastian Cantillo, Macarena Rubio; construction: Maya Harrison; engineering: Davide Tanadini; chair Prof. Dr. Elli Mosayebi, Lukas Burkhart, Theres Hollenstein, Matthew Phillips, Selina Puorger, https://mosayebi.arch.ethz.ch/en/models/

4   Jorge Luis Borges, "On Exactitude in Science" (1946), in: idem, *Collected Fictions*, trans. by Andrew Hurley, New York: Penguin Press, 1999, p. 325.

5   By canceling the distinction between model and depiction, Jean Baudrillard identified the lack of reference that characterizes signs today, speaking in this context of the "simulacrum." Jean Baudrillard, *The Agony of Power: Semiotext(e)*, Los Angeles 2010.

6   Completion, client: UTO Real Estate Management AG, Zurich.

7   The project is described as a "Performative Space," as, for instance, on the website of the Elli Mosayebi chair: https://mosayebi.arch.ethz.ch

8   El Lissitzky, "Wand-Mobil für Kommunenhaus," 1929, in: *Das neue Frankfurt*, Issue 11, 1930. Exhibited at the Dresden Hygiene Exhibition, 1930.

9   For spatial construction and process, see El Lissitzky and Lazar Markovic (1929), *Russland: Architektur für eine Weltrevolution*, Berlin/Frankfurt am Main: Ullstein, 1965, p. 24; Sigrid Loch, *Das adaptive Habitat. Typologie und Bedeutungswandel flexibler Wohnmodelle* (dissertation, Fakultät für Architektur und Stadtplanung, Universität Stuttgart, 2009), Stuttgart: Universität Stuttgart, Institut Wohnen und Entwerfen, 2011, p. 556.

10   Regarding this design of a 40-m² residential unit with sliding door and inserted separator, see also: Sigrid Loch (see note 9), p. 557.

VACANCY NO VACANCY
NINA ZSCHOCKE

vacancy – no vacancy: from July 2019 to March 2021, a pink neon sign on the roof of the ETH's Faculty of Architecture announced the availability of a small furnished habitat. The lettering marked a one-story structure on the southwest side of the roof terrace that could be tested for a week's stay. By day it was seen as a dark volume set off against the sky. Sitting on the roof like a little hat, the penthouse was made by the Elli Mosayebi Chair for Architecture and Design out of solid cross-laminated timber (CLT) and placed on top of the HIL building inaugurated in 1976.[1] An unclad façade signaled the temporary nature of the structure, with light-colored slats, visible from afar, that fastened down the dark waterproof tarpaulin. In contrast to the binary announcement outside, the interior of the unit contains elements whose position can be seamlessly adjusted by hand. A wall and a closet can be rotated as flexible room dividers and swivel lamps adjusted accordingly. Drawers and trapdoors for storage space are tucked into the platforms that separate two zones from the circulation area. Mattress and carpet distinguish these zones as areas for sleeping and living. Kitchenette and bathroom are fully equipped and functional. The apartment with its linoleum flooring and painted walls is ready for occupancy.

There is also a small balcony, delimiting a slightly elevated, covered area that ensures privacy on the roof terrace, otherwise accessible to ETH students and staff for informal use. The project has several names. One is *vacancy*, and another:

Mock-up.
The small prefabricated building was hoisted by crane up to its temporary location, where it rested on wooden rails, leaving a space between the structure and terrace roof. Its status was also ambiguous: full-scale model, model house, module, laboratory. The architects call it a "mock-up," that is, a sectional model for presentation that performs on several layers. Demonstration and test are closely related in a mock-up. It is made to persuade a future client, to demonstrate its positive qualities and also to serve as a means of exploring potential details of execution.[2] In contrast to façade elements frequently tested outdoors in this fashion, a complete habitat was presented in full-scale, including all interior fittings.

In fall 2018 and spring 2019, the chair at ETH Zurich had already produced full-scale models within the framework of teaching projects, implementing designs on

---

1   The HIL building on the ETH Hönggerberg Campus was built by Max Ziegler and Erik Lanter from 1972 to 1976.

2   The background in this case was a project planned by EMI Architects on Stampfenbachstrasse 131 in Zurich for UTO Real Estate Management AG: Performative House, by direct commission 2018, completed 2022, https://www.emi-architekten.ch/en/projects/stampfenbach/

NINA ZSCHOCKE

EMI

VACANCY NO VACANCY

EMI

EQUILIBRIUM IN MOTION

JOSEPH SCHWARTZ

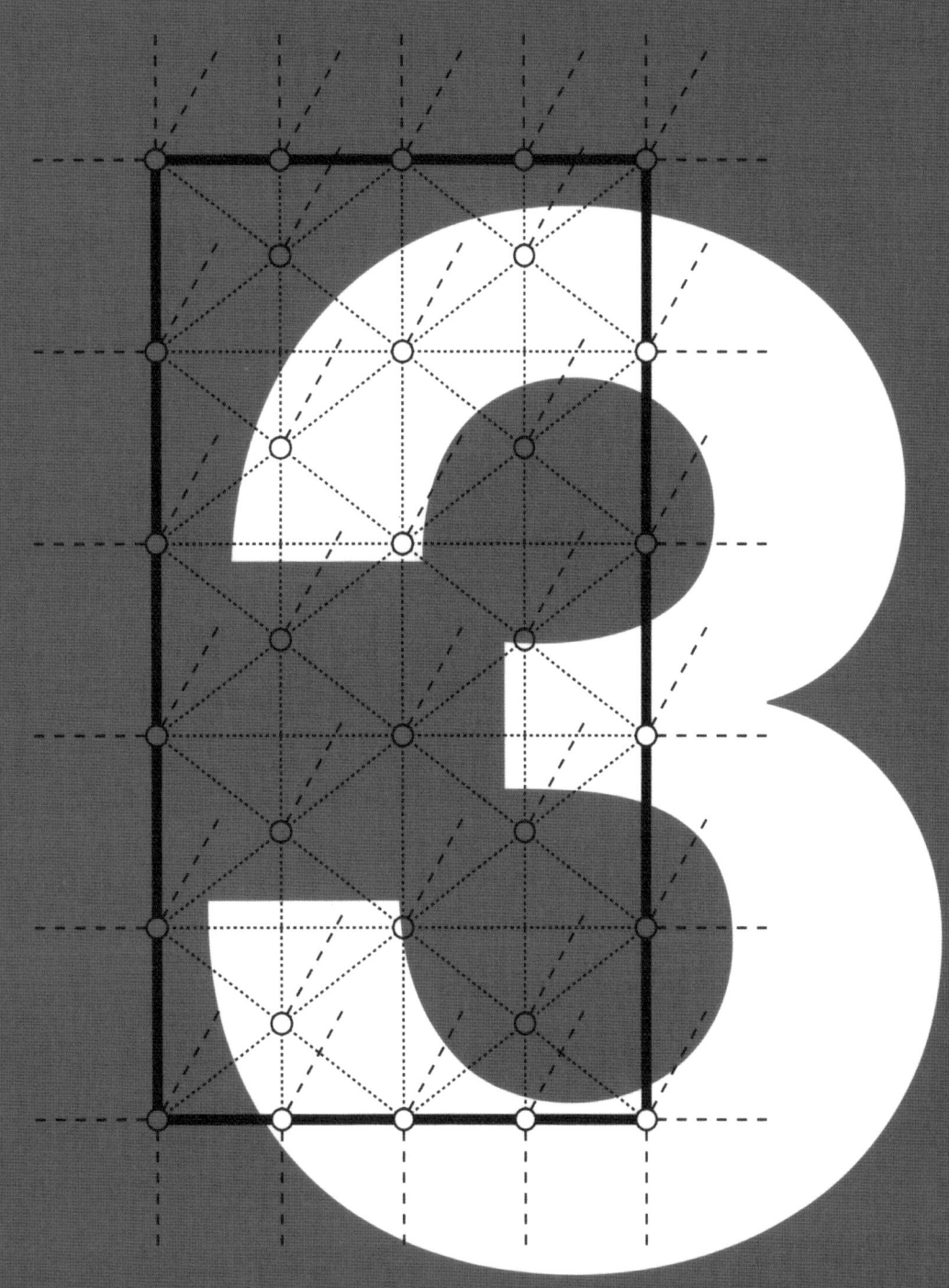

EQUILIBRIUM IN MOTION
JOSEPH SCHWARTZ

For the installation *Anthropomorphic Form* for the Swiss Art Awards 2019, EMI Architects, in collaboration with Fabian Bircher, drew on cable and membrane engineering. One surface of the room—the ceiling—was a textile membrane whose shape was changed by geometrically shifting the boundary conditions, i.e. its points of support. A translucent fabric suspended from cables aligned in five axes was set in motion using an algorithm that responded to various parameters of human and ambient activity in the space, such as noise levels, the number of people and their distribution, and the speed of their movements. By varying the shape of the ceiling, they generated a performance of the architecture of the entire space—very much in the spirit of EMI Architects' experimental work exploring the architectural potential of performative spaces.

Movable (infra-)structures are a special case in the field of structural engineering. The focus here is on equilibrium, and the movement of a structural element is often associated with the loss of equilibrium and thus the collapse of the load-bearing structure. Strictly speaking, however, this observation applies only to static equilibrium. It is obvious that in addition to statics, which is the branch of mechanics concerned with the study of forces acting on bodies at rest, the field of dynamics deals with movements and time-varying loads that cause accelerations and thus also movements. Dynamics is divided into the fields of kinematics, which describes only the geometry of the motion of bodies without considering the forces acting on them, and kinetics, which considers both the kinematics and the forces causing the motion. Unlike mechanical, ballistic, hydraulic, or thermodynamic engineering, dynamics often plays only a subordinate role in civil and structural engineering, with the clear exception of vibration and earthquake analyses.

In conventional structural calculations of rigid, stationary structural systems in civil engineering, the theories of both elasticity and plasticity formulate equilibrium on the undeformed system. Since one of the goals of the calculation, namely to ensure serviceability, is to keep deformations to a minimum, this simplifying assumption, which originally made the calculations mathematically solvable in the first place, is entirely justifiable. On the other hand, if deformations play an important role—for example, if they can be responsible for the collapse of the supporting structure—they must also be taken into account when calculating rigid systems. This is the case, for example, with stability problems such as buckling or bulging.

It is interesting in this context to note that equilibrium can be thought of as the prevention of uncontrolled motion. The Earth's gravity causes any body with mass to accelerate toward the center of the Earth, which is something that must be controlled or stopped. In the case of wind load, the flow of air

exerts suction and pressure forces on the surfaces of any body, which are influenced by the shape and surface properties of the body itself. These forces result in acceleration of the body, which must be prevented. For purely static problems, structural engineers must therefore ensure that movement of the load-bearing structure is prevented or, strictly speaking, kept within very narrow limits. To simplify matters, they simulate the effect of wind with so-called equivalent forces.

Dynamic problems are no different: here, too, the goal is to control the movements or keep them within limits. However, the equilibrium conditions are now formulated on a moving system whose motion must be controlled. This applies to oscillating, vibrating, floating and flowing bodies or media as well as those moving on land, water, or in the air.

During flight, an aircraft maintains a complex state of dynamic equilibrium: In terms of vertical equilibrium, the gravitational force acts against the aerodynamic lift force; if the former exceeds the latter, the aircraft sinks, if the latter exceeds the former, it rises. A horizontal force is required to propel the aircraft horizontally, and this is generated by the engines. The aircraft moves through the medium of air, which exerts additional (drag) forces on the aircraft, similar to the effect of wind on a building. Here, too, the shape and surface properties influence the forces acting on the aircraft both on a small scale (roughness of the material surface) and on a large scale (control flaps). In addition, the speed itself is a key parameter that significantly influences these forces. Thus, it becomes clear that a whole set of interacting parameters are involved in formulating the equilibrium conditions and thus in controlling an aircraft. This complexity can be felt in a mysterious way by the passengers, who are in an enclosed space that on the one hand gives them a feeling of safety, but on the other hand allows them to experience the aforementioned accelerations to which they are exposed during a flight, be it smooth or turbulent.

Civil engineers in the field of hydraulic structural engineering also deal with dynamic equilibrium. An example where the movement of the water is so slow that almost no dynamic forces are encountered is a navigation lock, which enables ships to overcome differences in water levels along a river. Here, the natural flow of the river is used to fill the lock chamber and empty it again. Since the water level in these chambers rises or falls slowly, the forces acting on the side walls and gates change progressively. The experience of passing through such a facility in or on a ship is impressive. There is something unnatural about the water surface impounded at the far end, creating an uncanny feeling as the ship enters the dark lock chamber from the lower end downstream and the gate closes behind it. As soon as the water level begins to rise steadily, the proportions of the chamber change and it becomes progressively brighter; the ship slowly emerges from the chamber, reconnecting with its surroundings, but at a new, higher level. If you are on deck during this process, various senses are stimulated: sight, hearing, smell, touch. When the ship enters the lock from upstream, it is the unexpected narrowness of the lock chamber, gradually revealed as the water level drops, that informs the performative spatial experience.

> Another important branch of mechanics is kinematics, which describes the motion of bodies in purely geometric terms with the variables of position, time, velocity, and acceleration. Kinematically permissible is a state of motion that fulfills the kinematic relationships and boundary conditions. For instance, a rod that is attached to an extremity with an axle-like pin can only move within the plane in such a way that the individual points of the rod perform circular movements. This is the case, for example, with the spokes of a wheel. The attachment of the axle determines the boundary condition, and the kinematic relationship results from the geometry of the (kinematically permissible) path of motion.

Bridges spanning rivers or lakes pose a particular hazard to navigation when they have little clearance above the water's surface. Civil engineers have solved the resulting problem in a variety of ways, including the use of lift or bascule bridges that allow ships to pass. Here, too, slow movements with low accelerations are involved, so dynamic balance plays only a minor role. Bascule bridges, in which the bridge span can be swung up in one or two parts thanks to hinges near the abutments, represent a pragmatic approach. London's Tower Bridge is a notable example. The operating mechanism poses high technical demands here, too, but the structure remains in an inherently conducive state when pivoted upward, waiting to be returned to its bridge-like state after the ship has passed. The situation is different for vertical lift bridges, where the entire bridge span over the nautical channel is raised translationally, usually by means of a cable drive mechanism. The Jacques Chaban-Delmas lift bridge in Bordeaux, which was completed in 2012, is an interesting example of how this great technical challenge can be met with a strong desire for creativity. When the lift span of the bridge lies just above the water's surface, connected to the approach bridges, the continuity of the bridge deck seems so strong that it is hard to imagine that this elegant structure is capable of transformation. The four vertical pylons, each 77 meters high, form a kind of landmark, like oversized milestones. When the lift span is raised to a great height, a completely new sort of structure is created: a towering, coherent gate structure that defines an unexpected new space for ships to pass through. The height of this space can be varied to accommodate ships of different sizes. This is made possible by the type of drive mechanism. It uses suspension cables that are redirected downward over sheaves at the tops of the masts and are attached to massive counterweights that can slide up and down inside the masts. Thus the structure is always in a quasi-unstable equilibrium, and only small drive forces are required to set the lift span into low-speed motion or to bring it back to a standstill.

Another lift bridge worth mentioning is the pedestrian bridge at the Jet d'Eau in Geneva, completed in 2016, which features a mechanism based on the scissor principle. Here, too, when in its horizontal state to allow people to walk or bike across the bridge platform, there is nothing to suggest that it is even possible for the span to transform into a shape that allows small boats to pass underneath. Only its massively oversized side guardrails with their unexpectedly articulated joints might suggest that the bridge harbors a secret. All is revealed at the moment when the bridge morphs into a wave-like shape, transforming the formerly flat platform into a staircase. This means the bridge can be used to cross the waterway in either condition: barrier-free in its flat state, or via the undulating stairs when raised. An interesting feature is the operating mechanism, which is actuated by pistons at both ends of the bridge. Instead of using cables to raise the span, as at the lift bridge in Bordeaux, deformation is introduced locally into the structure at both ends of the bridge by internal forces and then elegantly transmitted via the ingeniously arranged articulated scissor elements to create an evenly curved shape. The restricted kinematics not only control the outer profile of the bridge but also ensure that the stair treads retain their horizontality. This gives the structure a somewhat organic appearance—similar to a spine whose vertebrae, joints, tendons, and muscles allow its shape to change.

The load-bearing principles of lift bridges can also be illustrated using simple puppets. A marionette, for example, works on the same principle as a cable-operated lift bridge; the individual limbs are rigid and connected by joints in a way that allows certain movements while preventing unwanted ones. This determines the kinematics of the system. The motion itself is controlled indirectly by external strings, which are so delicate compared to the puppet itself that, even though they are perceptible, they give the object a magical facet. As soon as the figure moves, it comes to life and the strings fade entirely into the background. The skillful and practiced manipulation of the strings is what makes the puppet's movements seem so realistic and adds significantly to the fascination of the lifelike marionette. With a traditional "Punch and Judy" hand puppet, movement is controlled in a different way, directly by human fingers moving inside the puppet. This means that the kinematics of the puppet's individual limbs are also indirectly controlled by one's fingers, so the requirements for the rigidity of the puppet's individual parts are lower. This is closer to the mechanism of a system driven by internal forces, such as the scissor bridge.

The behavior is again different in the case of a segmented push puppet, where the individual elements are pretensioned with the help of thin rubber bands so that they are almost rigidly connected to one another. If the connections lose their rigidity by loosening the rubber bands

4

Anthropomorphic Form, Swiss Art Awards, installation, 2019–21, model studies showing shapes formed by the fabric

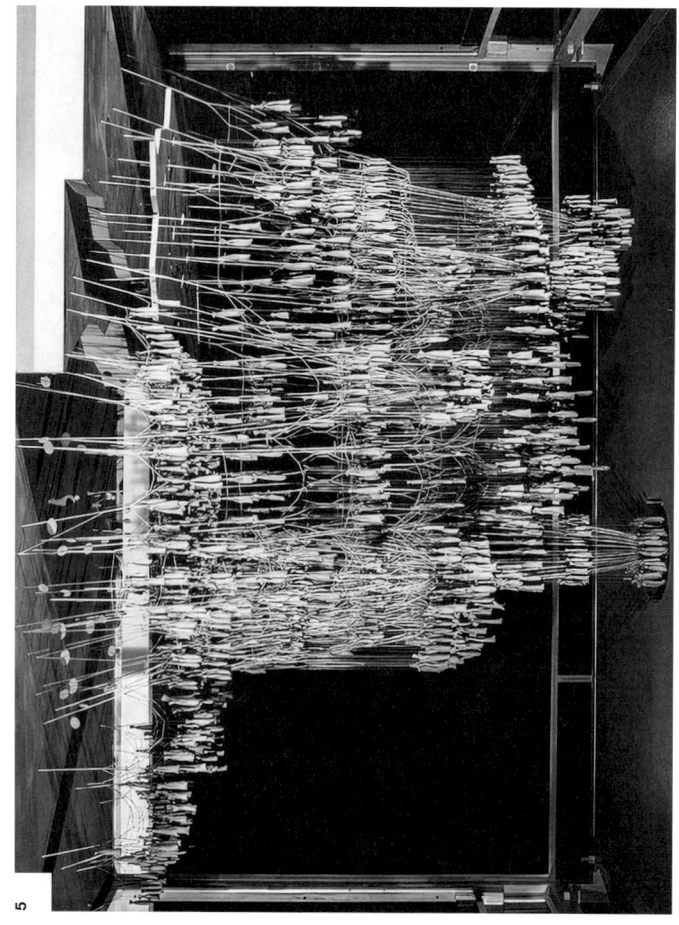

by pressing the spring-loaded button in the base, the manikin can be gradually put into a slack state and will straighten up again when the tension is reapplied. Due to the tolerance of the contact surfaces in the joints, the position of the figure can vary slightly in the tensioned state. The action imposed on the limbs by the inner connecting bands is similar to that of pistons.

Starting from the concept of a lift bridge, the planning team for the Swiss Pavilion at the 2016 Venice Architecture Biennale conceived a variable space in their first design, which was later rejected. The team investigated the extent to which the originally vertical and horizontal boundaries of a space can be altered by means of translational and rotational movements so that the perception of the space slowly changes. For reasons that included the complex technical implementation, the kinematic movement was ultimately abandoned in favor of a static, uncontrolled, unexpected, and random "movement" in a concave surface. The visitor's unfamiliar sense of orientation within the space is intensified by the uniformly white, seamless, and randomly curved surface under controlled lighting conditions and is in fact closely related to the perception of a space whose surfaces change kinematically.

Instead of moving the positions of the rigid surfaces of a room, as originally intended in the earlier design, it is more effective to work with flexible elements whose shape can be changed within the system.

> This leads to another interesting branch of mechanics, namely cable and membrane engineering, where kinematics plays an important role in the so-called form finding of the flexible load-bearing element. Unlike rigid structural members such as beams or slabs, cable and membrane structures can only accommodate internal tensile forces. Cables, chains, and textiles are important representatives of this structural category. They are often referred to as form-active systems because the form can adapt to the applied loads, but must also do so to achieve a state of equilibrium.

This principle was also indirectly at work in both the marionette and the Bordeaux lift bridge, but it was not the core theme. For example, the marionette can be viewed as a three-dimensional articulated chain whose elements consist of the limbs, the joints, and the strings. In the observations presented, however, the focus was on the rigid parts of the body, which are connected to one another according to certain kinematic rules. In the examples above, the strings and cables themselves were merely ancillary to the generation of motion, not form-active in the sense of being part of the supporting structure itself. It was not primarily the forces that dominated the derivation of form, but the boundary conditions of the kinematic states of motion.

The situation is different with cables and membranes, which have no flexural rigidity. Here, the cable or the membrane between the suspension points (i.e., the static

5 Reconstructed hanging model of the church designed for Colònia Güell (1898–1908) by Antoni Gaudí. The model was reconstructed in 1982 by the Institute for Lightweight Structures at the University of Stuttgart and the Gaudi Group at Delft University of Technology at the request of Kunsthaus Zürich for the exhibition *Der Hang zum Gesamtkunstwerk*.

6 Christian Kerez, *Incidental Space*, installation for the Swiss Pavilion at the 2016 Venice Architecture Biennale
Photographs: Oliver Dubuis

boundary conditions) is responsible for establishing equilibrium by adjusting its shape. Distributed effects such as the membrane's own weight lead to a distributed curvature, so that the deviation forces of the membrane under tension must compensate for its own weight at every point to ensure equilibrium. Concentrated forces acting on the membrane lead to a discrete kink in the cable or to a conical deformation in the membrane. It was recognized early on that the shape required for the equilibrium of a complex flexible system can be advantageously determined—or rather found—experimentally. By mirroring the shape found around the horizontal plane, the dual shape of a tensile membrane, namely that of a shell under pressure, can be derived. This is the way Heinz Isler generated the shape of his shells, and how Antoni Gaudí employed a similar process to develop the shape of complex stacked shells.

For their installation for the Swiss Art Awards 2019, EMI Architects, in collaboration with Fabian Bircher, drew upon cable and membrane engineering as a principle of form finding. Each momentary state during the ever-changing dynamic process thus represents a static state of equilibrium that experimentally determines the shape between the attachment points of the cables, which are moved by motorized winches. The magnitude of the forces in the membrane depends primarily on the respective deviations of the membrane between each attachment point. The lower the deviation, the greater the internal forces. The localized introduction of forces at the cable fixation points creates conical deformations with localized stress peaks, the consideration of which was critical to dimensioning the membrane and to determining the minimum deviations that had to be accommodated to prevent the membrane from tearing.

The richness of the shapes that were repeatedly generated in unexpected ways, especially in the progressive, algorithmically controlled change from one constellation to the next, impressively demonstrated the enormous creative potential of this process of form finding for the design of a performative space. Similar to music, where just a few notes can be used to create an almost infinite number of very different melodies, a membrane can generate a virtually infinite number of shapes based on the combination of qualitatively similar curvature values.

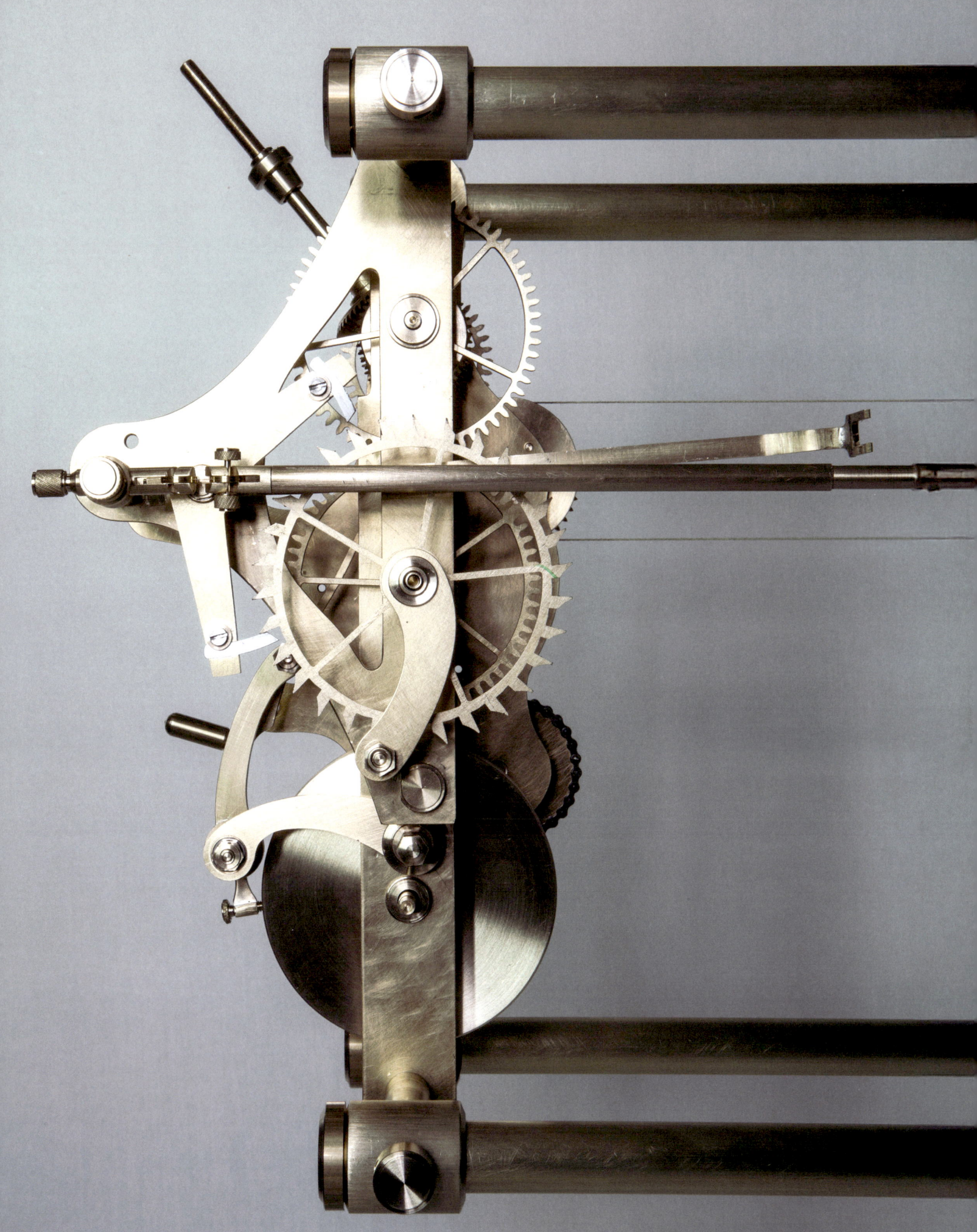

hours, that determine the rotation speeds of the platforms on the East Ridge. Mock-ups are used to measure and verify the statistics of movements and the implementation of individual components or parts of a building as well as the color effects of architectural elements. This all adumbrates an approach to architecture that is no longer solely restricted to a building and its construction but that also equally involves "performance" in terms of infrastructures, machines, apparatuses, and computers, and that—echoing the categories set out by the "mechanologue" Jacques Lafitte in his *Réflexions sur la science des machines*—no longer treats the building as a purely "passive" machine (e.g., a column transferring loads) but as one that is also "active" and "reflexive," insofar as it has the capacity both to transform energy streams and to adjust its own behavior depending on environmental influences.[8]

There is a correspondingly extensive range of expertise that—in keeping with the postulate of economies already stipulated by Lance—combines challenges from such diverse disciplines as sociology, astronomy, engineering, electronics, air-conditioning technology, and psychology, and gives all of these a visible, meaningful form through architecture. The rotating discs on the East Ridge that turn the building into an individualized experiential machine, the sensors in Basel that use an algorithm to process changing human activities and atmospheric conditions to create ever-new spatial effects, the doors and mobile furniture in Zurich that facilitate occupant-specific living: these not only reflect ever more refined technical and structural systems, they also open up realms of social practice that are increasingly differentiated and individualized. They illustrate a new cartography that renegotiates the relationship between technology and human beings, between private and public, inside and outside, the physical and the atmospheric, and that—as the few indicators in the drawings show—has already, little by little, largely come into being below the radar of cultural perception. The challenge now is to inform it with architectural meaning.

---

8   Jacques Lafitte, *Réflexions sur la science des machines*, Paris: Vrin, 1972 [1932].

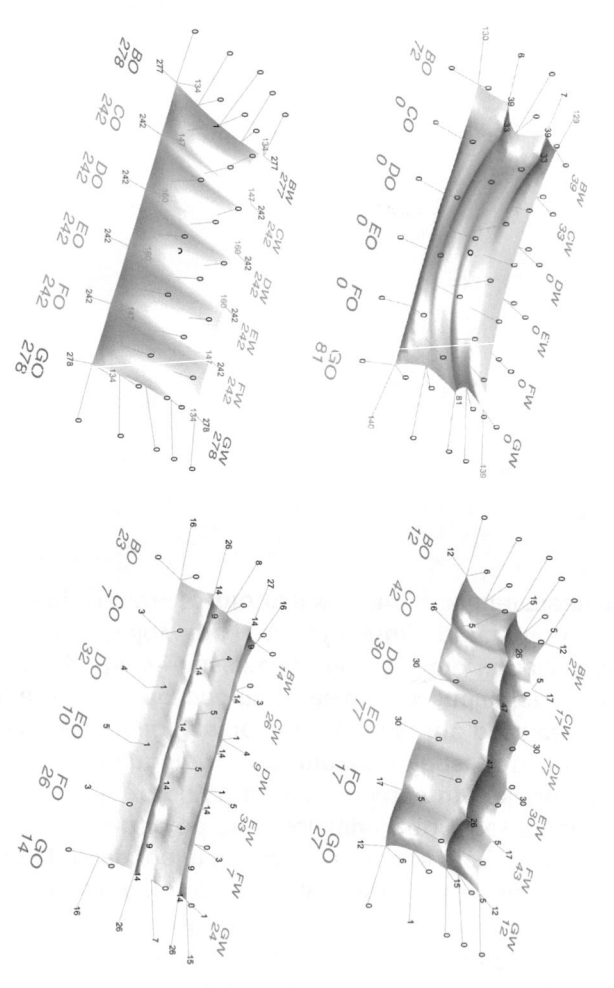

7

Anthropomorphic Form, Swiss Art Awards, installation, 2019–21, simulation of the dynamic forces created by different formations

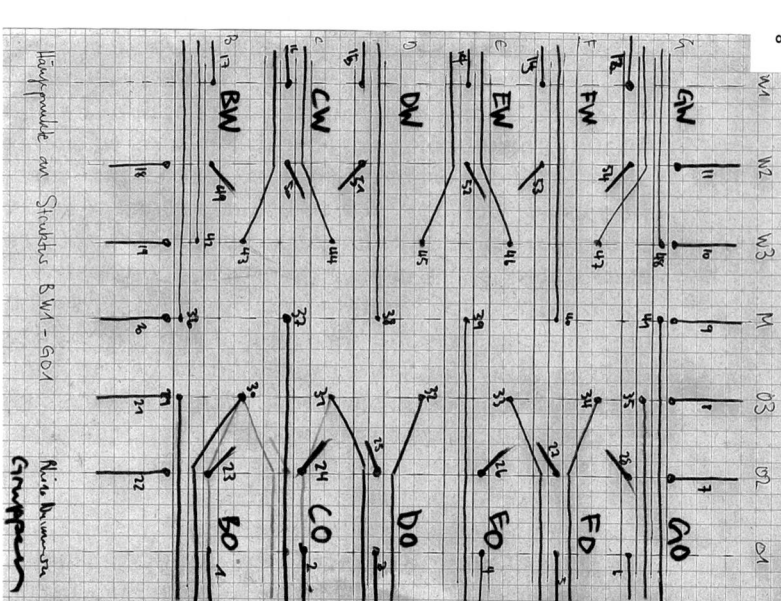

8

Anthropomorphic Form, Swiss Art Awards, installation, 2019–21, circuit diagram showing suspension points for the fabric

and activities. Flexibility is the watchword of modernism and post-modernism, driven by the desire to do justice to ever greater expectations of comfort, adaptability, and individualization. As EMI Architekt*innen have put it in a short explanation of their installation in Basel, the fabric ceiling in effect becomes "an organ of the visitors in the space" because the algorithms that set it in motion respond to "the actual behavior of human beings."

This goes hand in hand with demands for precise programming in floor plans. From the mid-nineteenth century until the onset of modernism, domestic floor plans were ordered according to various functions (dining room, living room, bedroom, etc.). However, after World War II they were increasingly ordered according to the activities that could take place, in various forms, within that space. During the course of the twentieth century separate rooms and passages—two basic features in nineteenth-century dwellings—gave way to more flexible layouts. This development came about (as Georges Teyssot aptly put it in his study of *The Disease of the Domicile*) in the hope of "rendering the inflexible flexible."[5]

Nowadays the distinguishing feature of a floor plan is above all its topological order rather than its geometric or structural properties. And this order is more readily apparent in projects with fixed or ephemeral remits. In the case of the East Ridge, for instance, the functioning of the system is determined by the mechanical interplay of pendulum, cog wheels, and in Basel there is a similarly essential coordination of electronics and mechanical devices: sensors and control center on one hand, cords, winches, and fabric on the other. And this can be seen just as compellingly—albeit mainly apparent during the design process—in the *Performative House* in Zurich, where the relationship between the shape of the plot, the placement of the crosswalls, the radius of the mobile structures, and the spatial concept are investigated and coordinated, step by step. A special part is played by secondary spaces (kitchens and bathrooms) and non-loadbearing partitions, which have to absorb irregularities in order to ensure the smooth interplay of the mobile structures. Besides the precise programming of the spaces, the focus here is on anticipating possible activities and any movements these may invite.

What these aims mean for the architect's approach to space was outlined, from different points of view, by Giulio Carlo Argan and Jacques Dreyfus. In the late 1950s Argan, an art historian, showed in his book on Marcel Breuer how walls—stripped of their function as spatial enclosures—had become furniture. The ensuing "domestic ambience" is now defined by built-in furniture and mobile partitions. Some years later, in his *System of Objects* Baudrillard also uses the term "ambience."[6] For Baudrillard, as it had been for Argan, the emphasis had shifted from the single object and its design to the interplay of individual items in ever-changing configurations. Twenty years later the French engineer, Jacques Dreyfus, took a different approach in *La société du confort* when he turned his main attention to air temperature, sound insulation, and humidity—in other words, the precise calibration of the atmosphere in a room.[7] Dreyfus's main concern in his digression on building regulations and standards is directed less at maximizing a room's flexibility than at regulating the environment within the space (enabling purely atmospheric flexibility). The room (a geometric entity) and the space (as a perceptual experience)—two central aspects of the design—are now "joined by" atmosphere (as both an aesthetic and technical category).

Ultimately it is within the confines of the architect's drawings (floor plans, elevations, sometimes axonometry, too) that these new forms of dwelling are negotiated. It is within drawings, which are by nature static, that new conventions—lines of motion or even arrows—are introduced to illustrate new requirements such as operativity and performance. Initially notation techniques of this kind were used to indicate the flow of water and air in homes or public buildings; they were subsequently also used to show the direction of travel of vehicles and pedestrians and to mark the movements of housewives in a kitchen—and other occupants and users later on. These arrows, as broken or solid lines, chart movements in space and time in otherwise static drawings. As design tools they allow the architect to anticipate movement. Whereas circulation routes in particular were planned and illustrated in the 1930s—take, for example, Alexander Klein's housing studies with clearly delineated routes—from the 1950s onward there was growing interest in visual relationships, the circulation of air, and structural forces. In the same way that the connections between pantry, kitchen, and dining room or between the cooker and the sink used to be precisely organized, in the postwar years—as in designs by Gio Ponti—careful planning went into the visual relationships between parents' and children's bedrooms, between entrances and reception rooms, kitchens and dining rooms or, more often, between inside and outside spaces.

As demands on architecture change, notations are becoming finer, more differentiated and more individual, but also less visual. "Metereological and astronomical" values (measured by sensors) are brought into play, as in the installation by EMI Architekt*innen in Basel, and as in the depictions of the patterns of movement arising from phases of the moon, from the passage of days and

---

5   Georges Teyssot, "The Disease of the Domicile," in *Assemblage* 6, Cambridge: MIT Press, 1988.

6   Jean Baudrillard, *The System of Objects*, trans. by James Benedict, London: Verso, 1996. First published in French: *Le Système des objets*, Paris: Gallimard, 1968.

7   Jacques Dreyfus, *La société du confort. Quel enjeu, quelles illusions ?*, Paris: L'Harmattan, 1990.

Machines

Although the notion of performance seems to be absent from architectural discourse in the nineteenth century, the concomitant operative aspect of architecture increasingly came to the fore as the century progressed: witness the successful integration of the metaphor of the machine into architecture. Although not the first to equate architecture to a machine (that had already been done by others such as the physician Jacques-René Tenon in 1788), the French architect and critic Adolphe Lance specifically used the term in the context of architecture. In 1853, at the end of a lengthy review for the *Encyclopédie d'Architecture* of the first volume of a new—"excellent," as he put it—architectural treatise by Léonce Reynaud, Lance expressed the hope that the second volume would deal in greater depth with processes that, thanks to advances in science and technology, could be useful in daily life. Lance felt that the idea of a house had changed: "A house," he writes, "is an instrument, so to say a machine that no longer serves to provide shelter for human beings but that, as far as possible, bending to the human being's needs, should support his pursuits and multiply the fruits of his labors."[3] In that respect industrial premises, factories, and workshops were exemplary and worthy of imitation. Even if this may seem an odd metaphor, the house is also a factory because that is where we generate countless private everyday acts. Lance writes that thorough investigation into this area could enrich our homes and daily lives with a wealth of benefits and assets.

This would, however, require a change of perspective: "Might it not be possible," the author asks by way of an introduction, "to contemplate an edifice or house not merely in terms of its arrangement and distribution?" The point of this would be—leaving aside formal matters relating to *disposition* and *distribution*—to discover the many new devices, the multiple aids, indeed economies in time and energy that new processes would have to offer. Lance thus placed the question of performance or operativity center stage long before the term had become part of the wider discourse on architecture.

This is exemplified in the increasing interest in issues relating to "circulation," which gradually ousted compositional considerations on the basis that architecture can have an impact on temporal and physical processes. As opposed to earlier assessments, the search for economies (as Lance puts it) was no longer restricted to the building alone but now took in all movements within the building, movements whose flow should be regulated, ordered, and modulated. From now on architectural drawings are seen as the place where the architect can anticipate various factors whose consequences need to be managed and contained: movement, sunlight, odors, noise, and so on.

Although Reynaud did not take the bait, Lance's concept of the house as a machine and the associated notion of performance became an enduring source of inspiration to architects and still define the historical and cultural context of architectural debate today. Over the years, against the backdrop of changing ideologies and evolving technologies, the notion of architecture as a machine has always entailed explaining its performance in terms of particular contexts and processes. These could be anything from construction, structures, building physics, usage, and space to programming and perception. Ultimately, regardless of semantic nuances, the "machinery" of architecture is not merely a production outcome: it is not only a material object, it is always also an action.

The text by EMI Architekt*innen on the *Performative House of the Future* seems like a contemporary response to Lance. The architects state that "The idea for this kind of living is rooted in the idea of a 'performative space' that adapts to each occupant." Individual architectural elements therefore have to be rethought: "Floors and ceilings, doors and walls, fixtures and furniture, windows, structural features, curtains, mirrors, and so on." The focus is less on the construction of components or the materials used for them than on their programmable variability: the floor should also be able to function as somewhere for sitting or lying down on or even as a storage space; meanwhile mobile furniture and structures such as doors, lighting, and cupboards guide movement within the space. Fixtures, components, and devices form a matrix, within which the various activities of individual occupants are both facilitated and regulated. A comparable, digital customization is seen in EMI's fabric ceiling in Basel, whose movements do not merely "respond to various parameters of (human) activity: noise levels, visitor numbers, the speed with which visitors move around, etc.," but also offer visitors a new experience each time they arrive.

Architecture

A range of different genealogies that contribute to the "performative space" can be identified. Firstly, technological: starting in the second half of the nineteenth century various features were introduced into architecture that aided the precise regulation of the flow of light, air, and people—conduits and devices that were the focus of Sigfried Giedion's study of mechanization in architecture,[4] as well as numerous other features that gradually reorganized internal spaces: sliding doors connecting rooms so that these can be used in different ways, as the need arises; glass walls that sink into the floor removing any threshold between inside and outside; or curtains that, more than other modern design features, reflect the increasing emphasis on the capacity to structure a space to suit particular times

---

3   Adolphe Lance, "Bibliographie. Traité d'Architecture, par M. Léonce Reynaud," in Victor Calliat and Adolphe Lance, *Encyclopédie d'Architecture*, vol. 3 (Paris: Bance, 1853), col. 68.

4   Sigfried Giedion, *Mechanization takes command: A contribution to anonymous history*, New York: Oxford University Press, 1948.

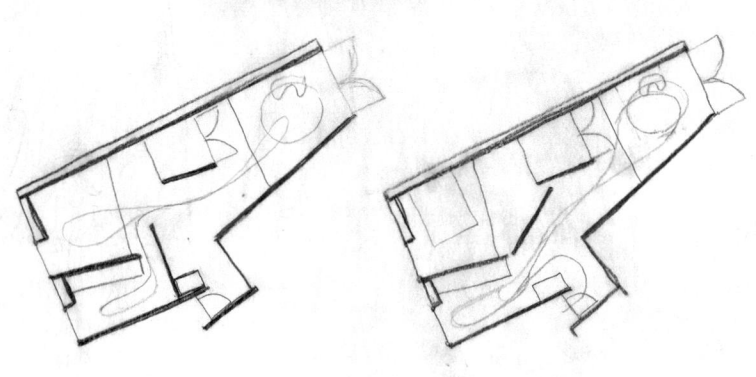

4

Apartment Building Stampfenbachstrasse, Zurich, 2018–22, sketch of the spatial relationships defined by the position of a movable wall

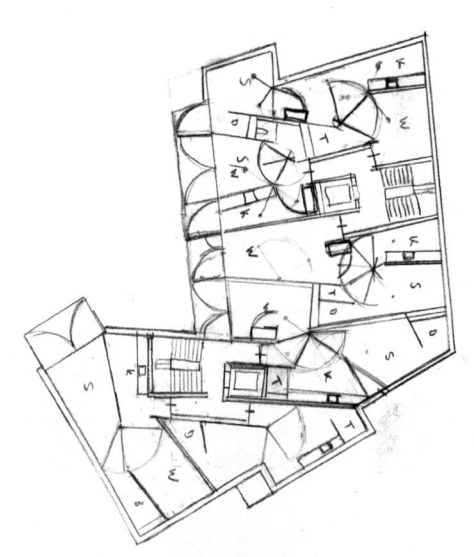

5

Apartment Building Stampfenbachstrasse, Zurich, 2018–22, sketch of the standard floor plan with arcs marking the movements of performative elements

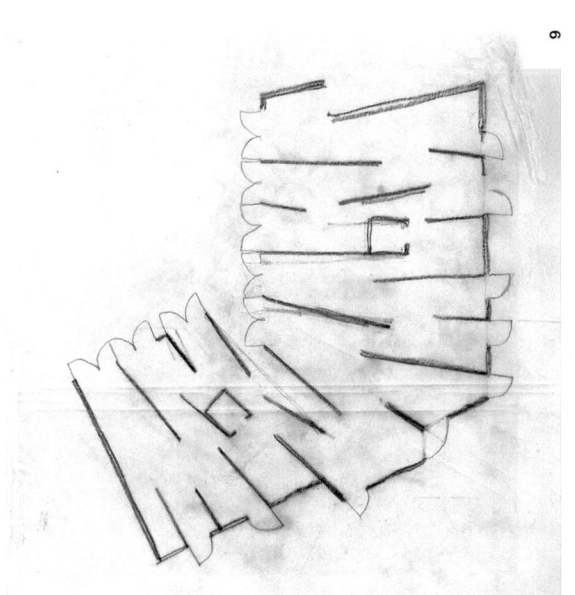

6

Apartment Building Stampfenbachstrasse, Zurich, 2018–22, early sketch of the "movable walls" of the supporting structure

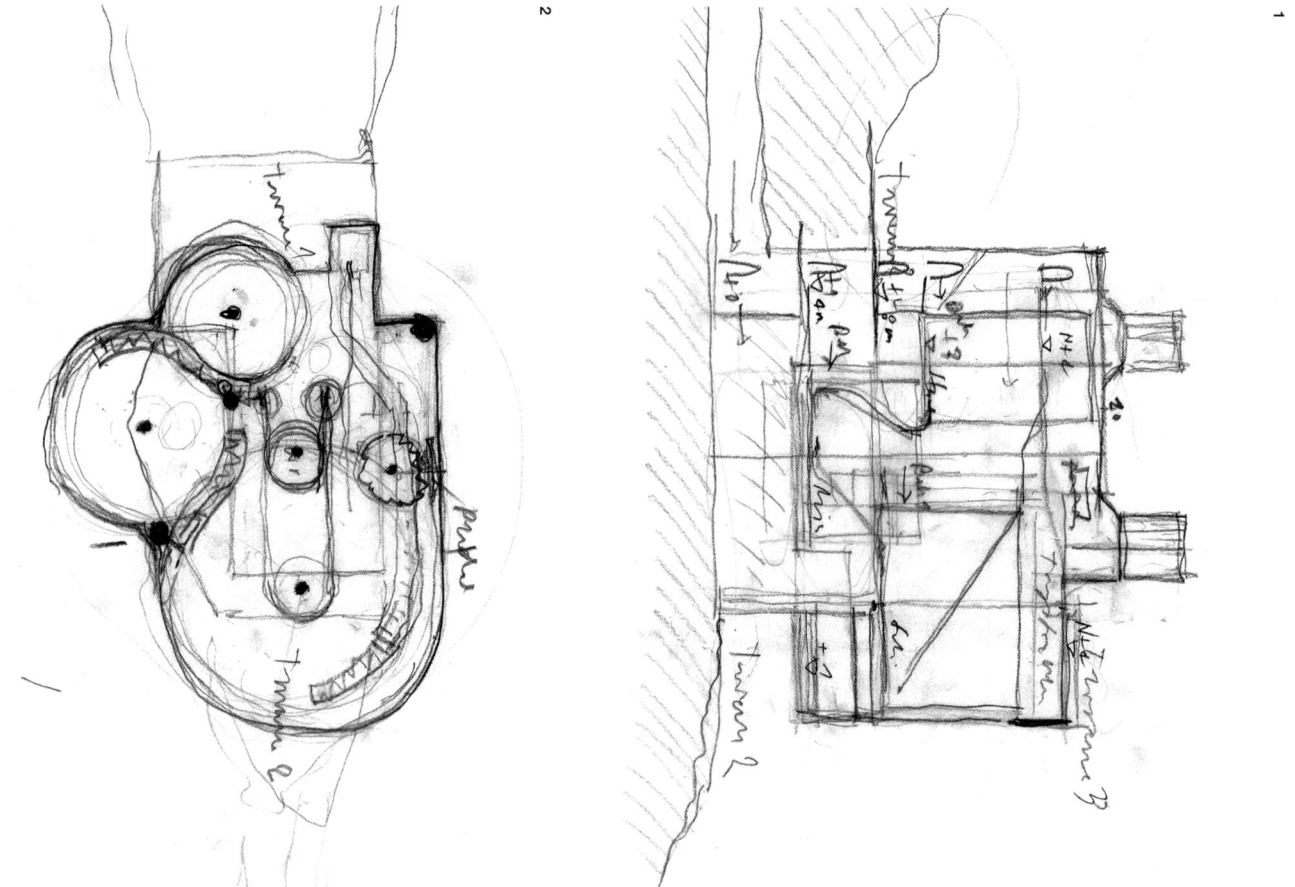
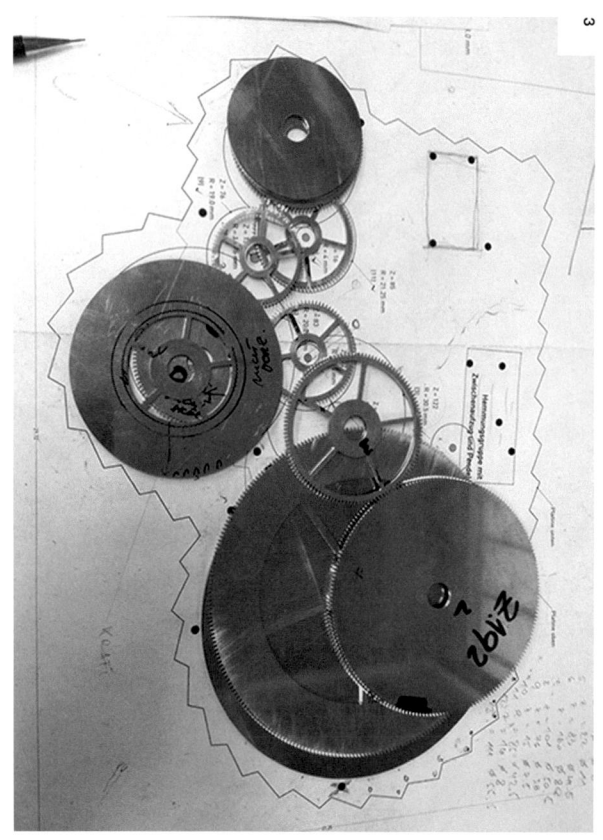

achievement as such. And in the early twentieth century—in the realms of technology in general and automobiles in particular—it was utilized in a similar vein in connection with the output of machinery and motors. In linguistics it refers to the production of language—as opposed to grammar, which defines linguistic forms. The term "performance" appears to be French in origin; however, after World War II, thanks to its English equivalent, it spread into disciplines as diverse as cinema, anthropology, art history, and sociology. In the theater and in the world of dance it is increasingly used in connection with a particular event or rendition. At the same time the meaning of the term has also expanded to include the achievements or efficacy of a person, a machine, or a system. In 1957, in an essay on the state of architectural theory in light of the increase in programmatic demands on architecture, the art historian John Summerson still used the term "performance" in its traditional sense, explicitly with regard to the way that architecture fulfills specific functions. In a special issue of *Progressive Architecture*[2] in 1967 "performance" is closely linked with new construction technologies and rationalization methods developed in the postwar years. Following a revival in the 1990s, it is now used to describe processes and procedures used in digital fabrication—and most recently it has been used in connection with sustainability and the energy rating of buildings. However, to this day in architecture the term "performance" has retained an element of ambiguity. It can be used both of the measurable quantitative "performance" of a building and its components, or, rather more loosely, in relation to the activities that take place within it.

Even if the technical affinity of the three projects by EMI Architekt*innen cited here could be disputed, interest in the performative aspect of their architecture cannot be reduced to that alone. Any exploration of the operative dimension of their work relates not only to individual moving mechanisms but just as much to furniture, architectural features, and layouts. A survey of the extensive collection of references that was assembled in preparation for these projects reveals references to apparatuses, vehicles, and devices from the realms of technology—a ball bearing (disassembled), a prototype Junkers aircraft from 1932, and a watch movement. The collection also includes celebratory architecture such as a stage set by Diller + Scofidio (for the Duchamp Centennial), Eduard Spelterini's balloon at the barracks in Zurich (1893), and a mock-up of Eero Saarinen's Gateway Arch in St. Louis (c. 1950), as well as architectural icons such as the façade of Frank Gehry's Spiller House (1980), the splayed supports in Kazuo Shinohara's House in Uehara (1973), and numerous floor plans—for the Burgtheater in Vienna, for instance, for Aldo van Eyck's Nieuwmarkt playground (1968), and Adolf Krischanitz's Traisenpavillon (1988).

2   *Progressive Architecture*: Performance Design, August 1967.

3
A Clockwork House, Jungfrau East Ridge, competition entry, 2012, 1st Prize, gear wheel blanks on a model construction plan in the workshop of watchmaker Miki Eleta

2
A Clockwork House, Jungfrau East Ridge, competition entry, 2012, 1st Prize, early floor plan sketch showing the positions of individual access and clockwork elements

1
A Clockwork House, Jungfrau East Ridge, competition entry, 2012, 1st Prize, early section drawing of the volumes, the interior, and the Savonius rotors on the roof

NOTATIONS
LAURENT STALDER

At first sight they may escape one's notice—the little arrows, delineating motion and forces that inhabit the drawings by EMI Architekt*innen. For all their discretion and sparing use, these marks challenge the standard depiction of constructions and spaces in traditional architectural drawings. In technical drawings for the *Clockwork House*—a tourist destination on the East Ridge of the Jungfrau—arrows indicate the direction and the rotation of the various discs and belts in this kinetic complex. The floor plans in the presentation drawings for compact three-room apartments in Zurich include radiuses and semi- and quarter-circle arcs that indicate the range of movement of doors, lighting, and items of furniture, prefiguring the potential partitioning of living spaces. In the installation elevations and floor plans for the fabric ceiling of *Anthropomorphic Form* in the Messehalle in Basel, the cords that support the fabric are rendered in different colors and illustrate the horizontal and vertical loads that impact the structure depending on the configuration of the ceiling. These discreet notations in EMI's presentation drawings are complemented by diagrams, schemes, and motion sketches. One such diagram shows the "forces, transmission ratios, and bearings of moving parts" and a scheme details "rotation times T, the peripheral speeds v" etc. of the transmission mechanism on the East Ridge. Among the drawings for the fabric ceiling in the Messehalle in Basel there is a "script for the different situations" of the ceiling geometry and a sketch showing the ceiling illuminated by cones of light from spotlights below it. In a series of floor-plan sketches for the Zurich apartments, the exact angles and exact positions of the walls of the apartments are worked out and a sequence of photographs of a mock-up of one home explores different spatial arrangements.

These references and symbols, notations and diagrams that are found in a variety of documents all anticipate different forms of movement and illustrate the ensuing operative dimension of the buildings in question. These marks come to fruition in the mechanical rotary movements on the East Ridge, in the computer-generated movement of the ephemeral tented fabric ceiling, and in the swing doors and other moving items in the *Performative House* with its "performative space," as the prototype for compact apartments in Zurich was called.

Performance
The use of the term "performance" and its root concept is, as Bernard Stiegler showed in his text "Performance et singularité" (2004),[1] a relatively recent development. It originally referred to the execution and completion of a task. In the nineteenth century it started to be used more widely, mainly by race goers in horse-racing circles. Here and subsequently it was used in relation to sporting

---

1   Bernard Stiegler, "Performance et singularité," in *La performance, une nouvelle idéologie?*, ed. Benoît Heilbrunn (Paris 2004).